SHIPS GONE MISSING

ROBERT J. HEMMING

CB

CONTEMPORARY
BOOKS

CHICAGO

Library of Congress Cataloging-in-Publication Data

Hemming, Robert J.
    Ships gone missing : the Great Lakes storm of 1913 / Robert
J. Hemming.
        p.   cm.
    Includes bibliographical references and index.
    ISBN 0-8092-3909-4 (cloth)
    1. Storms—Great Lakes—History—20th century.
    2. Shipwrecks—Great Lakes—History—20th century.
    3. Great Lakes—History.
    I. Title.
F551.H416   1992
977'.031—dc20   92-19576
                                                                 CIP

OTHER BOOKS BY
ROBERT J. HEMMING

Gales of November:
The Sinking of the Edmund Fitzgerald

Tales of the Iron Road
(with Maury "Steamtrain" Graham)

With Murderous Intent

Published by Contemporary Books, Inc.
180 North Michigan Avenue, Chicago, Illinois 60601
Manufactured in the United States of America
International Standard Book Number: 0-8092-3909-4

To
John R. Miller,
who said I could

Contents

Acknowledgments

I OWE A DEEP DEBT OF GRATITUDE to several people who contributed their time, effort, and talents to assisting me in the research necessary for this book:

Robert W. Graham, archivist at Bowling Green State University's Institute for Great Lakes Research, and his assistant Susan H. Riggs, for their help in compiling newspaper, magazine, and photographic material;

Elaine Blair of the Goderich (Ontario) Branch of the Huron County Public Library for her help in compiling local newspaper material;

To the staffs of the Sarnia (Ontario) Public Library, the Toledo/Lucas County Public Library, the Burton Historical Collection of the Detroit Public Library, and the Michigan Historical Collection of the University of Michigan I offer my sincere thanks.

A special expression of appreciation must go to my wife, Ann, for her tireless careful checking, editing, and correcting of the manuscript for this book. I didn't always take her suggestions, as any flaws that may remain in these pages will attest.

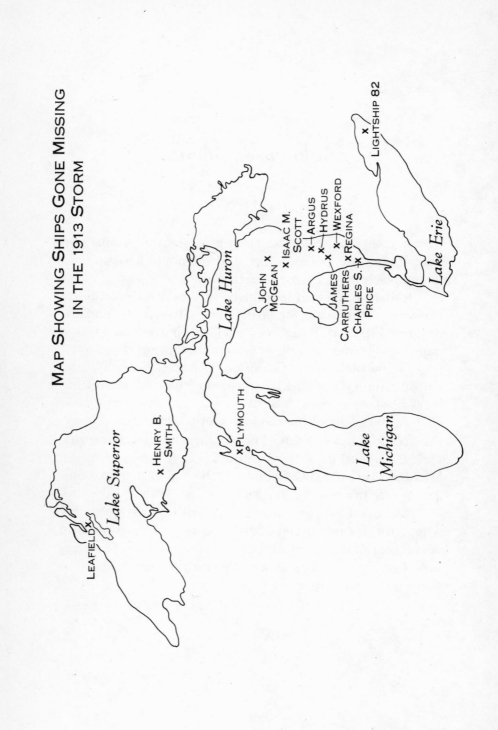

MAP SHOWING SHIPS GONE MISSING IN THE 1913 STORM

Lake Superior

LEAFIELD x

x HENRY B. SMITH

Lake Huron

x PLYMOUTH

JOHN McGEAN x

x ISAAC M. SCOTT

x ARGUS

x HYDRUS

JAMES CARRUTHERS x

x WEXFORD

x REGINA

CHARLES S. x PRICE

Lake Michigan

x LIGHTSHIP 82

Lake Erie

CHAPTER 1

A Prologue

FROM THE SURFACE OF THE MOON, they are the most instantly recognizable feature on the North American continent. They comprise the largest inland body of fresh water on the globe. They have been called the world's "eighth sea," and their bottom is littered with the wreckage of more than six thousand ships. They are the Great Lakes.

The gouging, scraping, and dredging of the five lakes began over one million years ago during the Pleistocene epoch, when four great glacial ages spread over the upper Middle West. The tumultuous process that formed the Great Lakes has never ended—it continues today.

To anyone acquainted with the expansive oceans of the world, the Great Lakes appear to be benign bodies of water, presenting no serious dangers to those who would venture out on them. But to those who have endangered their lives in a sudden and raging storm on one of the lakes, they are anything but calm and harmless.

The first recorded loss of a commercial vessel and her crew on the Great Lakes was also the first documented attempt to carry a cargo over these uncertain waters. In 1678, at the direction of French explorer René-Robert Cavelier, Sieur de La Salle, the Franciscan friar Louis Hennepin established the first shipyard on the Great Lakes for the purpose of building a cargo ship to carry furs from the western French territories of Lake Michigan to the eastern end of Lake Erie, where they could then be shipped from the Lake Ontario side of Niagara on to the Saint Lawrence River.

The shipyard was constructed on the east bank of Cayuga Creek in present-day Buffalo, New York, at a spot now named La Salle Park, in honor of the once-favored son of France.

The Seneca Indians watched in uneasy awe as the huge ribs of the giant "canoe" rose and the ship began to take form. She was sixty feet long, weighed between forty-five and sixty tons, and had five cannons mounted below her main deck. Her two square sails were ornamented with the fleur-de-lis, her prow with the armorial griffin—the fabled animal with the body of a lion and the head and wings of an eagle—the crest of the house of Louis de Buade, Comte Palluau de Frontenac. She was christened the *Griffon* as the blessings of God were pronounced over her bow and the men sang the "Te Deum" and fired a salute from her guns. The Indians watched in disbelief and then got drunk on French brandy. The newly launched ship was towed out into Lake Erie, and on the morning of August 7, 1679, she sailed west bearing trinkets for trading along the way.

The trip across Erie was serene, and La Salle, resplendent in a ceremonial cloak and plumed hat, stood at the rail marveling at the lush greenery, abundant game, and wild fruit lining the shore.

North through a narrow river that the French explorer dubbed *détroit* ("the straight," which would later give the Motor City its name) the *Griffon* sailed, La Salle still commenting on the beauty of "this fertile and pleasant" waterway.

On August 12 the ship moved out of the river and into

a lake. It was the feast day of Saint Clare and La Salle named the non-Great Lake in honor of the abbess of Assisi. Adverse winds required that the crew move onshore and pull the *Griffon* through what is now the St. Clair River and into the fast-flowing funnel of water at the site of present-day Port Huron, Michigan, the gateway to Lake Huron.

The second day on Huron dawned with the sky hazed in high cirrus clouds, the perverse harbinger of malevolent weather.

The storm struck late in the day, first a squall blowing with a sudden anger out of the northwest, slamming into the *Griffon* head-on and catching her master and crew unwarned. The ship was mauled viciously by the raking winds while the men aboard, helpless against the unfamiliar peculiarities of the storm, fell exhausted to their knees, hurling their prayers to the wind, calling out for a merciful God to deliver them from extinction. In a characteristically human attempt to bargain with a seemingly wrathful Jehovah, many in the crew joined in a common vow to make Saint Anthony of Padua the patron saint of this embryonic voyage on the lakes and to build a chapel in his honor, if only the wind and waves were stilled.

Only a man named Lucas, the vessel's pilot and an experienced ocean navigator, demurred at divine entreaty, choosing instead to curse and revile La Salle for having brought him to this humiliating end in a "nasty lake" rather than to an honorable death on a noble sea. The storm, as Great Lakes sailors would later come to expect, ceased as quickly as it had begun, and the *Griffon*, with her worn and wondering crew, sailed in idyllic weather up the lake and into what is now the Straits of Mackinac—their frantic promises to Saint Anthony unanimously forgotten.

The *Griffon* put into Saint Ignace, where La Salle

went ashore to kneel and quietly pray over the spot, under the floor of the crude log chapel, where lay the bones of Jacques Marquette, the Jesuit missionary who had founded the mission at the site eight years before. A week later, La Salle sailed the *Griffon* into Lake Michigan and down the western shore to Green Bay, where he made contact with his advance party, who had been sent months earlier to select and purchase the finest beaver, mink, and muskrat pelts the Indian and French trappers could supply.

On September 18, 1679, the *Griffon*, loaded with a fortune in furs, sailed out of Green Bay, headed back for Niagara.

La Salle, infected with exploration fever, remained behind with a small party, planning to go looking for the headwaters of the Mississippi River. As he watched his ship disappear below the eastern horizon, a smile of satisfaction crossed his thick Gaulish lips. He had gambled heavily on this venture, borrowing against his property at 40 percent interest. But, he thought as the *Griffon* sailed away, it had been worth the risk. He had won! Or so he thought.

Back again into Lake Huron the ship and her still disgruntled pilot, Lucas, went. And again they were pounced upon by a violent storm. It is not known whether the crew members attempted to renew their unfulfilled contract with Saint Anthony. What is known is that the *Griffon*, her crew, and all their valuable cargo vanished without a trace. To this day the hulk remains the quest of countless divers and historians.

There are those, however, who claim the ship still wanders the lakes, a freshwater *Flying Dutchman*, condemned to sail forever, never making port, and skippered by a man who eternally curses La Salle for bringing him to "this nasty lake."

And there are those who will tell you that, during the

howling winds of a Great Lakes storm, they hear the anguished cries of sailors in distress, shouting a word that sounds like *Mayday* but in fact is the French *m'aidez*, "help me!"

Since 1679, there have been hundreds of terrible storms on the lakes. Thousands of commercial vessels have been lost and countless crew members have drowned or frozen to death in these malignant waters.

The costliest single storm in terms of ships and crews lost occurred in November 1913 and is arguably the worst storm ever to strike the Great Lakes. It began on November 7, continued for four full days, and before it had blown itself out had swallowed up twelve ships, seriously damaged twenty-five others, and taken the lives of between 250 and 300 men and women. What follows is the true story of that awesome storm and of some of those who became victims of it.

PART I
ON SUPERIOR

CHAPTER 2

"The Season of the Wrecks"

"HEAVY WEATHER," AS STORMS ARE CALLED, cause concern to Great Lakes mariners at any time of year. But as autumn approaches apprehension grows, and when the month of November comes to the lakes, shipmasters begin anxiously searching the skies. It is axiomatic among Great Lakes mariners that with the eleventh month will come the storms and gales, and so too the cold, ice-making temperatures from the north. Then it will be but a matter of weeks before the lakes will start to congeal, to curdle in a white mass that begins first along the Superior shoreline, smearing outward, feasting on the open water, growing thick and swelling closer to the center with every frigid, wind-scourged day until it meets and joins with the ice from other parts of the lake in a three or four month union.

Time becomes vital when November crawls upon the lakes. Each additional load picked up and delivered means added revenues in the shipowner's treasury, added prestige and a good report in the shipmaster's personnel file, a few more dollars in the crew members' pockets, and a happier Christmas for all. And so they throw the dice "one more time," gaming with nature. Usually they win the throw. But the stakes in this game are immense, and when they lose, the price is often excessive. "Getting in a few more trips" has cost the life of many a whimpering sailor.

9

The Great Lakes pose several special problems to the mariner. With ninety-five thousand square miles of water, storing heat all summer, the lakes become their own weather factories when the cold polar air in autumn drifts over them, absorbing the heat on the surface in an upward explosion that is replaced with cold, driving winds—the gales of November. Storms on the Great Lakes erupt with a vicious suddenness that, prior to the introduction of radio communication and modern weather forecasting, frequently caught mariners unprepared, seizing their fragile vessels in a fatal grip, wrenching and twisting them in mountainous waves striking more swiftly and more frequently than any ocean crest. It is a seafarer's aphorism that saltwater sailors, disdainfully viewing the lakes as little more than inland pools, gain a devout respect for the Great Lakes once having survived a "heavy blow" on one of them. It is not unusual for experienced ocean sailors to become violently seasick in lake waves that have a different, more disturbing motion than those of the earth's seas.

Although the lakes are huge, there is often little maneuvering room for the boats because of the shallows that are found in many spots. In a strong blow, the lake boats—they are never called "ships"—dare not heave to and drift until the storm blows itself out, as can be done on the larger oceans; should they attempt this, the sailors would soon find their boats drifting on the rocks.

And each of the Great Lakes reacts differently in a storm: Lake Superior, with its barren, cheerless, rocky coastline and its killing cold water, has a deserved reputation of fathering the most intense, most deadly November storms. But the Big Lake is nonetheless preferred by many seasoned skippers in a storm because its depth throughout affords more maneuvering space than any of the other lakes. Lake Michigan and Lake Huron claim the lion's share of wrecks in the gales that sweep down their lengths, piling towering waves that have thundered out of the wretched black of night to smash to the bottom many a hapless ship and her screaming crew. Lake Ontario, which comes close to equaling Superior in depth, is generally the most benign of the lakes. It is Lake Erie, the shallowest of the Great Lakes, that stabs the sailor's heart with icy fear. For even on a beautiful summer day, when the surface appears as hard and polished as a spacious mirror, a sudden squall can churn those waters into savage madness that can hammer and smash and suck the unprepared vessel below the maelstrom to later vomit bodies and bits of wreckage along its verdant shoreline.

The design of the lake boats also offers particular problems for master and crew in stormy weather. They have been fashioned to carry bulk cargo: coal, iron ore, and grains. Consequently, they are long and slim. A typical lake boat in 1913 had a forward deckhouse consisting of a bridge or pilothouse, quarters for the captain, first, second, and third mates, and deckhands. On the large freighters there might be a crew's lounge and, in some cases, cabins for passengers and guests. This structure was usually positioned as far forward as possible.

Behind the deckhouse was a long, low deck called the spar deck. This area contained numerous hatch covers which, when removed, allowed the positioning of cargo in the massive holds in a controlled fashion.

At the stern was another deckhouse, which contained the galley, officer's dining room, often a captain's private dining room where he could entertain guests, the crew's dining room, and quarters for cooks, stewards, engine-room personnel, firemen, oilers, and coal passers.

The only means of reaching these two deckhouse "islands" was by crossing the long spar deck. In bad weather, this journey could be extremely hazardous as icy waves washed over the low freeboard of the deck. On modern lake boats, tunnels connecting each end of the boat and running along either side just below the spar deck provided cover and protection for crewmen making the trip from fore to aft.

The boat was built with a narrow beam to allow it to pass through canal locks such as those at Sault Ste. Marie, and a shallow draft allowed it to safely navigate the rivers and harbors around the lakes. This flat-bottomed, canal-boat design made it highly unstable in the deep wave troughs created in Great Lakes storms; a boat finding itself broadside in a deep wave valley could find itself heeling hard over and in danger of capsizing.

The positioning of the bridge, almost over the bow-sprit, was designed to provide larger deck space to accommodate additional hatches. But it also allowed huge, powerful waves and tons of water to crash over the prow and up to the pilothouse. In an extreme storm, many a steering crew found the windows crashing in with the full force of the seas swamping them. It was not unheard of to have the pilothouse itself torn away and washed overboard.

Following seas were capable of inflicting the same sort of damage to the after deckhouse. In addition, sky-lights were susceptible to being smashed in, sending a Niagara of water down on the "black gangs" and engine-room crews and frequently causing damage to the propulsion machinery.

Because of the often forced isolation of the steering crews and the propulsion crews, there had developed a sense of independence between the two groups leading to a jealously guarded "division" of command between the ship's master and the chief engineer. "You run your end of the boat and leave me to run mine," was a frequently heard demand during disagreements between the two superiors.

Those who "worked the boats" were less like seamen

than they were like blue-collar workers; they had a job to go to during each of their watches, much as a factory worker travels to a plant daily. The trips they took aboard the freighters rarely lasted more than a few days, which brought them frequently into port. Many had wives and families in one of the towns and cities along the lakes, permitting them to be at home for a day or two every week or so.

There were layoffs during the winter that made possible extended time with friends and family and perhaps a vacation trip. The pay was quite good, considering that a sailor's food and living quarters were provided, and many of the men were able to save a modest sum during the shipping season.

In times of good weather, the lake-boat sailor had a relatively pleasant life with comfortable quarters, time to relax and read or write or play cards, and the best food and as much of it as they could hope for.

But when the skies turned gray and threatening and the winds began blowing from the north and the temperatures began to tumble, the lot of the Great Lakes sailor became much less attractive.

As early as October, it became evident that the dying months of 1913 would be stormy and violent.

On October 21, 1913, the Toledo *Blade* reported that a "number of boats at various ports were held up because of winds so severe" that the wooden steamer *Norwalk* had been driven ashore at Presque Isle in Lake Huron, stranding her thirteen-man and one-woman crew on board. In Superior, the steamer *Lackawana* had to be towed into Duluth after her rudder had been carried away by the fierce waves. From Fort William, Ontario, came reports that several vessels arrived covered with ice. The steamer *America*, upbound to Duluth, was fifteen hours overdue.

The heaviest October snow since the terrible storm of 1908 struck Lake Superior with temperatures dipping to a record eighteen degrees above zero.

In Lake Erie, the 273-foot-long wooden vessel *C. W. Elphicke* was driven aground and broke in two before sinking. Her eighteen-man crew was rescued.

In Cleveland, replicas of Christopher Columbus's three famous boats, the *Pinta*, the *Niña*, and the *Santa Maria*, which had toured the Great Lakes during the summer of 1913 and had been scheduled to sail for San Francisco, were towed into the harbor for safety.

A shipping record for the Great Lakes had been set in September, leading many to anticipate a heavy traffic volume in the closing months of the season. The inherent dangers to shipping in the waning months of the year prompted one area newspaper to editorialize:

> The season of wrecks upon the Great Lakes is near at hand. It comes in with the October gales and reaches its climax when in the upper lakes the spray freezes upon the rigging, and the shores and lights in the lower lakes are obscured by fog and rain. Probably four-fifths of all the disasters written in the chronicles of the lakes occur in this period.
>
> There has been less tempting of fate in the last few seasons of navigation than there was in the era of prosperity closing with 1907. But that temptation may be revived this year, for we observe by the reports from the Soo that a new record in traffic was made in September, indicating a busy season to the end of navigation. We trust that shipowners may be advised to let the fat charters of the closing days of the season go, that they may not let the chance for big profits

persuade them to match lives and property with the ice and wind and the freezing spindrift. The toll of the wrecks is quite large enough to satisfy even the sailormen who like to pit their endurance and skill against the elements.

Neither the writer of that editorial nor the citizens who read it could have known that the warning it contained would go unheeded with the most frightful consequences.

CHAPTER 3

"Find Something to Grab"

JIM BURKE FELT POORLY, SUFFERING the effects of a severe chest cold. He'd not been well for several days. Now he was becoming increasingly convinced that he was coming down with pneumonia and wanted very much to be home in Cleveland, Ohio, under his wife's tender care.

But on Friday, November 7, 1913, James Francis Burke was in Marquette, Michigan, aboard the ore freighter *Henry B. Smith*. Burke was the *Smith*'s second mate and felt a strong sense of obligation to his skipper, Captain Jimmy Owen, who was then experiencing his own private agonies. Jimmy was afraid he was about to lose his command.

On the same day, in Cleveland, where Jim Burke longed to be, another Great Lakes sailor, Milton Smith, assistant engineer aboard the 524-foot ore boat *Charles S. Price*, had a nagging urge to be somewhere else and was seriously entertaining the possibility of calling it a season right there in Cleveland.

"You're crazy, lad," Chief Engineer John Groundwater said when Smith mentioned that he might leave the boat before the end of the season. "We'll be tied up for the winter in a couple more weeks; if you stay you'll get your bonus on top of your pay."

Smith couldn't explain it, but there was a gnawing inside him that was driving him to leave the boat while the leaving was good.

16

On Lake Ontario, John Thompson was pondering how he would let his parents know that he had left the *James C. Carruthers*, a new and very attractive berth, for a much less appealing assignment on a rusty old coal hauler. He knew that his father would question his decision and young Thompson was silently practicing his arguments for this seemingly irresponsible action. But he wasn't terribly satisfied with the explanation he planned to give; if the truth be known, he didn't really know *why* he had left the *Carruthers*. It had been a spontaneous decision made on the spur of the moment.

Oh, well, he thought, he'd have to tell them sooner or later. His boat was scheduled to tie up in Toronto on Sunday. He would telephone home then . . . perhaps.

Up and down the lakes, other men—and women— were leaving or joining boats unexpectedly or for no good reason.

The eleventh month of 1913 had entered softly, carried on gentle southerly breezes that brought unseasonably warm temperatures to the upper Great Lakes. It had been in the high sixties in Duluth, and on November 6 the thermometers at the Soo Locks registered a high of seventy degrees.

"Damn strange weather for these parts," John "Spike" Noble, master of the steamer *Cornell*, told his wheelsman as they steamed around Whitefish Point, headed west and empty, upbound for Marquette, Michigan, and a load of iron ore.

"Maybe it'll stay like this for the rest of the season," the wheelsman said in an expression of supreme optimism.

"Not likely. Superior's never nice for very long, not in November. It'll turn nasty, you can bet on it."

The wheelsman shrugged. It was all the same to him; bad weather came with the territory.

The men who sailed the lakes held a fatalistic disdain for weather—good or bad—and suspicion of the men who forecast it. To them, these people were little more than meteorological tea-leaf readers.

"I don't know why the government bothers to have us up here" was a frequent complaint of Alexander G. Burns, station chief of the U.S. Weather Bureau at Sault Ste. Marie. "These damned sailors pay no attention to us. If you put up a storm warning at Nantucket, the boats stay in port until the storm blows out. On the lakes, they take a look at the weather forecast and then forget it."

As November drifted through its first seven days, an intense low-pressure system, which had developed over the Aleutian Islands, had begun moving across the Canadian provinces. A second large low-pressure cell had gushed over the Rocky Mountains and was swirling high above the plains states, sucking up heat and moisture as it moved, headed for lower Minnesota. The two systems would collide on Friday, November 7, 1913, over Lake Superior, spawning a savage storm that would grow and intensify and would then be fed by an unheard-of third weather cell up from the Caribbean developing into a five-day storm that would be remembered as the worst ever to hit the Great Lakes.

In 1913 reporting weather conditions throughout the United States was limited to the telegraph. Commercial radio broadcasting would not appear for more than a decade. And while all U.S. lifesaving stations, newspapers, and most Great Lakes shipping company dispatch offices were connected in a telegraph chain, the boats on the open water were left with nothing more than light and flag signals and shouts through megaphones to communicate with other boats and nearby shore installations. Radio telephones would not be seriously considered for lake boats until 1937.

Out of sight of land and other boats, mariners were as

isolated and helpless as if they were stranded on the moon. Frequently, boats and sailors of that period disappeared without a trace, their fate never fully learned. This was to be the case with a number of boats that found themselves on the lakes during the second week of November 1913.

At ten o'clock Friday morning, on telegraph orders from weather bureau headquarters in Washington, D.C., H. H. Richardson of the Duluth weather office hoisted a square red flag with a black square in its center. Immediately below the gale warning flag was a white pennant, a signal that indicated a storm from the southwest was imminent. At the same moment, duplicate warnings were being raised elsewhere along Lake Superior, at the Soo, at Whitefish Point, Grand Marais, Munising, Marquette, Houghton, Ashland, and other harbors along the south shore of the huge lake. Similar storm warnings went up throughout the lakes.

Boats already out on the lake began to discover for themselves that a "big blow" was coming.

Downbound in Superior was the Northern Navigation Company's 321-foot passenger liner *Huronic* on the season's final run between Sarnia and Fort William, Ontario. The line offered a seven-day cruise with Ontario stops in Sault Ste. Marie, Port Arthur, and Fort William aboard one of three sister ships. The white-hulled and black-trimmed vessels were the largest propeller-driven cruise ships on the Great Lakes. Six decks tall, each boasted staterooms for 562 passengers, all with running water and some with full baths, some with beds instead of berths, a dining saloon on the observation deck seating 272, barber shops, smoking rooms, buffet bars, music and writing rooms, and several observation rooms that doubled as ballrooms. The ships were models of opulence just nineteen months after the plushest liner of them all—the *Titanic*—had plunged to the bottom of the North Atlantic with more than fifteen hundred passengers and crew.

This late in the season, the *Huronic* was returning with just fifty passengers and thirty-one staterooms occupied.

Franklin and Betsy Field had chosen to take the cruise at this particular time of the year for two reasons: the sixth of November marked their fifth wedding anniversary, and the cost of the final week-long cruise of 1913 dropped more than 25 percent on November 1.

Franklin had paid $56.66 for the trip, which included passage in one of the best staterooms, all their regular meals, and rail transportation from their home in Windsor, Ontario, to Sarnia, where they caught the boat. However, as low as that price seems by present-day standards, it constituted almost three weeks' salary from Franklin's job as manager of a clothing store in Windsor.

"The trip was gorgeous," Betsy remembered. "The weather couldn't have been nicer; it was eighty degrees and sunny when we got to the locks."

But the winds were freshening as the *Huronic* steamed out of Port Arthur shortly after 11:00 P.M. Thursday heading for Duluth. By 2:00 P.M. Friday, the *Huronic* was pounding through a heavy chop on a westerly course for Whitefish Bay in light winds from the southeast. On the bridge, Captain Malcom C. Cameron, a grizzled forty-eight-year veteran of the lakes, watched the sky with a suspicious gaze. At sixty-two, he had suffered the vagaries of November weather on Lake Superior enough times to know that the largest of the inland seas could become vicious with little or no warning. As a young deckhand on sailing vessels he had spent many a terrifying hour chopping ice from the rigging and clinging for his life as monstrous boarding seas swept over him, attempting to break the puny hold he had on the lifeline and drag him into the foaming maelstrom. He had experienced the awesome winds sweeping out of the northwest, cyclonic winds that snapped masts and spars as if they were twigs and crushed deckhouses as if they were strawberry boxes.

As Cameron watched his attention was drawn to the northern horizon.

"Starboard your helm," he ordered the wheelsman.

He had made the course change because of what he had seen in the lake to the north—or, more precisely, because of what he had *not* seen. There were no *Christmas trees*!

As the seas on the lake grow in size, the winds tend to cause the tops of the waves to spread out in ragged triangular patterns, which from a distance look very much like a continuous row of fir trees. Hence the term *Christmas trees*. When the winds increase sharply and beyond a certain speed, the force on the waves blows the tops away, leveling them off. Cameron knew that the winds several miles distant had suddenly shifted and increased considerably in speed. The heavy, rolling seas were moving with it, and they were heading his way.

The lumbering liner had barely managed to come to its new heading when a blast of wind and seas assaulted her head-on. The wind seemed to instantly rise to gale force, shaking the superstructure and burying the bow in a mountain of water.

To lookout Donald McCarthy, standing near the back of the wheelhouse, Cameron shouted, "We're in for it now, bucko. You'd better find something to grab."

Below decks, the passengers, many of whom had just finished a late and leisurely lunch, were now lounging in the reading rooms or the bar or, as Franklin and Betsy Field were, in the after observation room on A deck, considering whether to look for one of the couples they had met on the cruise and invite them to a game of cards, or perhaps instead to return to their cabin for a short nap.

"The first wave struck the ship so hard, I thought the

observation windows were going to crash in on us," Franklin recalled later.

Douglas Smitthers, an executive with the Packard Motor Company in Detroit on his first cruise, had just stepped out onto the promenade deck, preparing to take an after-lunch stroll around the ship.

"A sudden gust of wind caught me, tore my hat from my head, and threatened to pick me up and carry me over the side," he reported later. "At about the same time, I saw a wall of water strike the front part of the vessel and cascade down the deck toward me. I barely had enough time to grab hold of the nearby handrail and pull myself back to the door and inside before it struck me."

Beatrice Morvac, of St. Thomas, Ontario, was traveling with her recently widowed grandmother, Mrs. Arnold Rainey. Loretta Rainey had not wanted to come on this cruise. She had been haunted by the memory of a distant cousin who, early in 1912, had taken her first voyage at sea, a trip to America from her native Ireland. The cousin had regrettably found herself aboard the RMS *Titanic*. As one of the steerage passengers, she had not been allowed on the boat deck until the last lifeboat had departed. Her body had not been found.

"I felt that such a cruise would be therapeutic for her sagging spirits," Beatrice would insist. "I was told we would meet a great many fine people who would be socially acceptable and intellectually stimulating for her."

The next three days would certainly qualify as "stimulating."

Back on the bridge, Captain Cameron was experiencing his own brand of stimulation. The winds were lashing at the ship and the mounting seas were shaking her as a dog would shake a rag. Rigging wires were snapping and bulkheads were quivering and creaking and rivets were popping like firecrackers. The men on the bridge were seriously considering the possibility that the ship would come apart.

Through the rest of the daylight hours, Cameron and his crew struggled to keep the *Huronic* headed into the wind and waves, which was difficult in the extreme.

"There were many times when the wind would come from one quarter and the sea from another," First Mate Felix Winchell would later tell a maritime board of inquiry. "We wondered whether we'd be rolled over by the hurricane or capsized by the monstrous sea."

At about 2:30 Saturday morning, with the force of the wind continuing to build, the forward windows on the bridge suddenly exploded inward, carrying the window frames and other debris in with them.

"Get some men up here to clear away this destruction," Cameron ordered First Mate Winchell.

Crewmen arrived with axes and hacked and chopped away the remaining wood and metal framing. Then, standing amid the shards of glass and splinters of wood and metal, the captain and his wheelsman continued the struggle to keep the ship from foundering while the terrible gale raged around them.

A middle-aged woman seized the ship's purser by the arm and implored, "Sir, what is to happen to us?"

With a remarkable lack of tact or sensitivity, the purser replied, "Madam, I fear that we are about to be drowned."

To one of the stewards the purser urged, in a change of heart, "Tell your passengers that the captain is making for Whitefish Bay and that we will be safe from the storm there."

"Is that true?" the steward wanted to know.

"I've been so informed by the second mate. But I wouldn't give a copper for our chances of making it."

To another passenger, he said reassuringly, "The

worst that will happen to you, dear lady, is that you may have difficulty keeping your dinner down."

Strangely, given the ferocity of the storm and the pitching and heaving of the ship, none of the passengers reported the slightest trace of seasickness throughout the long and terrifying voyage. Apparently cold fear had suppressed all other senses.

The seemingly endless night dragged on. The horrified passengers, each having donned life preservers, huddled in the lounges, afraid to wait in their cabins lest an order to take to the lifeboats would pass them unheard. They gasped and moaned as each gust of the howling winds clutched at the ship, sending shudders through the decks beneath their feet. The winds flirted with sixty miles an hour, and the waves, bashing against the sides of the ship, at times reached a height of more than twenty feet.

The ghastly vision of the mortally wounded *Titanic*, plunging beneath the icy surface of the sea, taking with her a thousand and a half screaming, thrashing souls, paraded before the *Huronic*'s fearful passengers, who were now convinced they were about to suffer an identical fate.

"How could such a thing happen on a goddamn lake?" a man cried in anguish and disbelief.

At about the same time the *Huronic* was suffering its first assault by the growing storm, the steamer *Cornell* felt the first crash of the sea and tremor of the winds slamming into her. She was about ninety miles out of Whitefish Bay, returning from Marquette with a full cargo of iron ore. Through the day and into the night, Captain Noble battled the best nature's forces could throw at him as his boat plowed ahead, trying to make Whitefish Bay and safety.

But a combination of coincidence and bad judgment put the boat and crew in deadly danger.

At about 2:00 A.M. Saturday, the *Cornell*'s first mate

suddenly took ill. To assist in getting the mate below, Noble turned his boat before the wind, running with his stern pointed into the gale. When the mate was safely in his cabin and Noble ordered his vessel brought back to face the waves bow-on, he discovered that she would not fully respond; they became trapped in the troughs and in constant danger of being capsized. For the next thirteen hours, wallowing in thirty-foot valleys, rolling dangerously, every loose object in the cabins and the galley careening from the bulkheads, the crew fought—and prayed—to keep the boat from going over.

By late Saturday, the boat had been driven broadside to within a mile and a half of the Deer Park Life Saving Station on the Michigan shore. In an effort to get her bow around and into the wind and seas, Captain Noble ordered both anchors dropped and the engine run at full throttle ahead. At the same time, the crew ran oil through the hawsepipes in an attempt to smooth the heavy seas and allow the boat to gain headway. When the *Cornell* finally began turning she was even closer to the rocky shore with less than eight fathoms of water beneath the keel.

She would hold fast to the bottom for another twenty-four hours, her engine running at full speed the whole time. Her exhausted crew had been sleepless for more than a day and a half.

All across Superior more than a dozen boats struggled in the storm. A few managed to straggle into safe harbor early and simply wait out the blow. Others, caught far out in the lake, were at the mercy of the tempest. More than half would make it through with minor damage, several would be wrecked on the rocks and shoals. Two would vanish forever.

CHAPTER 4

"You've Made Me Lose My Boat!"

AS BAD AS THE STORM HAD BEEN in the early hours of Saturday, November 8, it grew considerably worse as the morning wore on.

The winds, which had thundered out of the southeast and then the southwest through the night, suddenly swung wildly to the northwest, continued growing in intensity for a couple of hours, and then, as quickly as before, veered out of the north pushing black mountains of water before them.

Accompanying the change in the wind came a rapid drop in the temperature, and with that came the snow: swirling clouds that struck the ships' wheelhouses like fusillades of buckshot combining with the wind-borne spray to build ice four and five inches thick on the windows.

Every surface of the rolling, twisting vessels on Lake Superior became fertile ground for a growing, swelling mantle of ice that congealed and distorted masts, davits, lifeboats, handrails, ventilators, and ladders. The ships became distended and heavy with the ever-growing weight upon them.

In this fiendish turmoil the *Cornell, Huronic, Turret Chief, Utley, George Stephenson, Fred G. Hartwell, J. T. Hutchinson, A. E. Stewart, Hydrus, Maricopa, Har-*

26

monic, Saronic, Sarnian, B. G. Berry, and the *L. C. Waldo* all struggled to stay afloat, to stay alive in the grip of the most vicious storm any of the shipmasters or crews had ever experienced.

Out there, too, somewhere in the black of Saturday night, were the ore carriers *Peter White, James C. Carruthers*, and *Leafield*.

Along the southern edge of Superior near the Michigan port of Munising and Grand Island the black-hulled Cleveland Cliffs steamer *Peter White* wallowed in gigantic seas, fighting to keep out of the troughs and find her way through the blinding snow.

Captain James Kennedy had brought the vessel through the Soo Locks at 5:00 P.M. Friday empty and northbound for Marquette to pick up a load of iron ore. When the terrible winds had hauled around to the north at about 3:00 A.M. Saturday, Kennedy decided to seek shelter. Headway was difficult to maintain without a cargo to give the *White* stability. The ship rode so high that waves passing beneath her stern had her propeller (or "wheel") out of the water as much as in, causing the engine to race dangerously, which required the chief engineer to work the throttle back and forth to prevent undue strain on the engine. While this saved the engine, the forward movement of the ship was slowed so much that every wave striking the ship's bow caused her to fall off her compass heading five or six degrees. Captain Kennedy found it necessary to constantly call for "hard a starboard" after each wave struck.

At about 6:00 A.M. Sunday, after thirty sleepless hours, with the crew approaching total exhaustion, the *Peter White* was nearing Grand Island when the snow abated considerably and the first signs of Sunday's dawn glowed lightly in the east. Kennedy, still battling the relentless winds, looked for a safe approach to Trout Point, where he planned to anchor in the lee of the land and await the end of the blow.

William J. Brown, the *Peter White*'s second mate, urged Captain Kennedy to make for the narrow passage between the Pictured Rocks and Grand Island. Kennedy was not enthusiastic about such an approach because of the strong winds and waves, but Brown argued that with the improved visibility, movement through the passage would be quite safe and would get them to the calm waters much more quickly.

Although skeptical about the maneuver, but too weary to disagree, Kennedy ordered the wheelsman to steer for the passage.

Just as the ship neared the narrowest, most danger-ous point in the passage, and too late to alter course, the snow returned heavier than before, totally obscuring the view of the men in the wheelhouse.

Certain that his ship was to be impaled on the rocks, the weak and wearied captain snatched the cap from his head and threw it to the deck and jumped up and down on it while screaming at his second mate in frustration and fury, "Now you've made me lose my boat!"

Within a minute, as suddenly as it struck, the snow stopped and the vessel was headed exactly on its course, easily clearing the passage.

To the northwest, near the tip of the Keweenaw Pen-insula, which juts into Lake Superior, the Bay Transporta-tion Company's 337-foot ore carrier *L. C. Waldo*, with a twenty-two man crew under the command of Captain John Duddleson, was trying desperately to find shelter in the lee of Manitou Island.

The vessel had departed Two Harbors, Minnesota, bound for Cleveland with a load of iron at 10:00 A.M. Friday, two hours before the storm warnings were raised. She had been struck by the first thrusts of the great storm into the lake. First it smashed in her wheelhouse windows, then it ripped away the roof, demolished her compass, and destroyed the ship's electrical system. Finally, a huge sea struck head-on and wrecked what remained of the wheelhouse in an explosion of wood and metal. Duddleson, his first mate, Charles Keefer, of Toledo, Ohio, and wheelsman Bernard Foley, twenty-nine, of River Rouge, Michigan, barely escaped with their lives by diving down a companionway into the captain's bedroom, which had already been devastated by the raging seas.

Taking only a moment to catch their breaths, Duddleson and Keefer made the terrifying journey across the open deck to the stern of the *Waldo*, where the emergency steering apparatus was located. With the mate holding a small compass and lantern, Duddleson struggled with the wheel, navigating by instinct and prayer.

Below, in the engine room, the men fought to keep headway as the ship rolled and pitched in the raging waters. As had been done aboard the *Peter White* to save the engine, the throttle was shut down each time a wave raised the propeller out of the water. But the efforts of the engine-room crew and those of the captain and first mate became futile at 3:00 A.M. when the writhing seas suddenly snapped the rudder from the ship, leaving the *Waldo* helpless in the frenzied waters of the lake.

An hour later the crew felt first one jolt and then a series of more bone-jarring concussions as the *Waldo* was driven onto Gull Rock near Manitou Island. Now the wind and waves went to work on the topside structures of the ship, smashing the after cabins and slamming at the weakened hull.

"My God, we're goners," Duddleson shouted as wave after wave smashed into the boat. The *L. C. Waldo* was a dying ship, and those aboard her knew it.

"I told Captain Duddleson that we couldn't stay at the stern," Chief Engineer Al Hacke remembered later. "I said that I thought we should move forward because the after hull was beginning to break up and I thought we'd have a better chance in the bow."

Duddleson agreed. The problem, however, was how to go about moving forward. The ship was being relentlessly hammered by twenty- and thirty-foot waves and swept by howling winds that drove sheets of blinding snow at speeds approaching sixty miles an hour. The hull was showing signs that it might come apart at any moment. There was no direct, protected access to the forward part of the vessel; it would be necessary for the crew members to go on deck and make their way to the bow with only the wire-cable railings running the length of the deck to use as a lifeline. It meant holding fast to the cable and inching along the more than three hundred feet in the teeth of the gale with the frigid waves threatening to pluck them from the deck and cast them into the killing seas.

The twenty men, along with two female members of the galley crew, began the hazardous trek forward. The women—Mrs. Alma Rice, forty-three, and her daughter, Mrs. Joan Mackie, twenty-seven—were paralyzed with fear and had to be literally carried by the men.

It took a full half hour to reach the forward deck-house, and upon arriving they discovered that none of the cabins had been spared the terrible battering the wind and waves had visited upon the ship. Everything was awash, with all windows gone and many entire walls missing. As they surveyed the wreckage in the bow, they felt the ship lurch and heard a grinding, tearing sound from the stern half. Looking around they saw the spar deck part halfway down the hull and sag heavily into the lake. The engine room flooded quickly and sank deep in the water. There was no way back. Duddleson and Engineer Hacke made a quick exploration of the portion of the *Waldo* still above water and discovered that the windlass room remained dry and sheltered from the icy winds.

Cold, wet, and miserable, the crew huddled in the small room. Two crew members, recalling that the crew's forward washroom had a bathtub, tore it from its moorings and dragged it into the windlass room. Several others ripped wood paneling from the captain's stateroom, furniture from his office, the wooden frame from around the bulletin board, and every other combustible they could tear loose. Carrying the materials back to the rest of the crew, they built a fire in the bathtub. The fire helped warm them, saving them from hypothermia and certain death, but the smoke choked and blinded them.

As they were passing through the galley on their way forward, Al Hacke had spotted two one-gallon tins of what he believed to be vegetables. He'd quickly grabbed them and managed to carry them forward. Now the famished crew opened the tins. The first tin proved to contain green peas while the second yielded peaches in a thick, sweet syrup. Cold, wet, and ravenous, the crew crouched over the bathtub for what heat it could supply, gasped against the choking smoke, and took what nourishment they could from their meager food stores.

Through the long and bitter night they prayed the storm would cease, horrified at the prospect that the pitching and heaving bow section would be pulled from the rocks and sink into the savage lake.

At dawn the weary crew discovered that, although navigating blind, Captain Duddleson had brought the ship within a few hundred yards of a sheltered anchorage off Gull Rock. In the quiet refuge they could see, through the heavy snowfall, the outline of another vessel. Occasionally the snow would let up and those aboard the stranded and wounded *Waldo* were able to see movement on the decks of the other ship.

"Find something we can hoist as a signal," Duddleson

ordered, and three men immediately rushed about until they located one of the ship's signal flags, which they quickly ran up the foremast.

In his cabin aboard the steamer *George Stephenson*, Captain A. C. Mosher had been sleeping after a frightening night battling the storm. Upbound and light, the *Stephenson* had been caught in the same sudden shift of wind that had surprised the other ships on Superior Friday night. For thirty hours Mosher had maneuvered his vessel through thirty-foot waves, roaring winds, and blinding snow, finally making safe harbor in the lee of Gull Rock, where he ordered all anchors dropped in twelve fathoms of quiet water. Now, at dawn on November 9, he was awakened by the first mate, who reported a steamer grounded on the western tip of Manitou Island.

"She appears to be abandoned; there are no lights and we can't see smoke from her stack," the mate stated.

As the sky grew brighter, the men in the *Stephenson*'s wheelhouse could see why no lights or smoke were present: from almost amidships, the beached steamer was broken in two with the after section half-submerged and the forward portion on the rocks and covered with a thick coat of ice, looking for all the world like a Great Lakes iceberg. But it quickly became apparent that the hulk had not been abandoned; as they watched, a distress flag slid slowly up the foremast.

"Hoist an answering signal," Mosher ordered. "And prepare to send a shore party to notify the Eagle Harbor Life Saving Station."

Help would soon be on the way to the beleaguered crew of the *L. C. Waldo*, but it would be many long, torturous hours before a rescue party would actually reach them.

A few miles to the north, another hapless crew had

watched helplessly as their ship was thrown upon the rocks.

The 257-foot Canadian Lake and Ocean Navigation Company's *Turret Chief*, under the command of Tom Paddington, rammed ashore on Keweenaw Point, five miles east of Copper Harbor, Michigan, just a few miles from where the *L. C. Waldo* had been systematically destroyed by the fearsome forces of nature.

Built in England, the *Turret Chief* had been converted and brought to the Great Lakes to transport grain and ore from the Canadian ports of Midland, Passage Island, and Fort William, Ontario. The little steamer was a solid and well-designed ship that gave competent service to her owners. Not so her skipper, Tom Paddington, nor her first mate, Joseph Phillips. During the ferocious November storm of 1913, their navigation was so atrocious that it caused the Dominion Wreck Commission of Canada to "severely censure" the two mariners for "incompetence that endangered her crew and caused the loss of their vessel."

There had been no storm warnings flying when the *Turret Chief* steamed out of Whitefish Bay on Friday morning. But by Friday night, the ship found herself in the midst of a storm so violent that she was literally spun around several times while heavy seas smashed open her pilothouse door and burst her steam lines.

Captain Paddington would later admit that after a few hours in the storm he had no idea where he was. He knew only that the wind and the seas were taking him south. But the befuddled captain took no action to maneuver against the drift that was driving him steadily toward the shore. When asked later why he didn't steam in an easterly direction that would have taken him into open water, the captain merely shrugged his shoulders.

Driven almost a hundred miles from where he had

estimated his position to be, Paddington found his ship propelled over two reefs and into a nest of boulders with her bow practically out of the water. She struck about four o'clock Saturday morning, and the crew quickly discovered that by dropping a line over the prow of the ship they could easily lower themselves to the rocks and make their way to shore.

Unlike the unfortunate crew of the *Waldo*, there was no shortage of food. The twenty-two-man crew of the *Turret Chief* was able to carry an adequate supply of provisions ashore with them, where they set up a crude shelter made from tree branches and prepared to wait out the blizzard that was then lashing the Keweenaw Peninsula. But after three incredibly miserable days and nights of drifting snow and ice that coated the ship with an estimated fifteen hundred tons, the men determined that they were in dreadful danger of perishing from the elements.

Under the questionable navigation skills of Captain Paddington, the crew began a painful march out, looking for some sort of settlement. They were not aware at the time that Copper Harbor was but six miles from where the ship had gone aground. By luck more than skill, they headed in the right direction.

Meanwhile, on the heaving lake, out of sight of land and beyond hope of rescue, there were others who were not as fortunate.

To the east, an hour's sailing time from the safety of Whitefish Bay, the *William Nottingham*, with three hundred thousand bushels of grain in her holds, was being mauled terribly by the monstrous, seemingly unending storm. Running before the gale, the long freighter was taking extreme punishment from the following seas that boarded her from the stern with a terrible regularity.

Her master, Captain Louis Farwell, a veteran of thirty-two years on the lakes, had attempted to confront the storm bow-on. But to maintain headway required that her engine be run at full throttle. While the heavily loaded ship rode reasonably well in the mountainous seas, the cost in fuel used soon became a source of serious concern to both Farwell and Chief Engineer Billy Stevens.

"Lake storms rarely last more than a few hours," Farwell would later comment. "But that one went on for days and days. There didn't seem to be an end to it. Our coal was being used up very fast and we weren't getting anywhere."

Hauling around to run with the storm again, Farwell decided to make a dash for Whitefish Bay before the fuel ran out. But it soon became obvious that they had waited too long. With only a few tons of coal still in the hoppers, Farwell and Stevens held a hasty conference. To run out of fuel while still at the mercy of the storm was a guaranteed death sentence, and they now knew that there would not be sufficient fuel to get them to safety. What to do?

In desperation the captain ordered the crew to strip away the tarpaulins over the wooden hatch covers and to open the aftermost hatch. Organizing a bucket brigade, Farwell had several hundred bushels of wheat in the hold moved to the coal bunkers to be fed into the fireboxes. The steam gauges reacted quickly and power was maintained until the *Nottingham* managed to crawl into Whitefish Bay, where she was thrown into a sandbar off Parisienne Island.

The seas, moving down from the north through the slot in the bay entrance, continued to assault the stranded *Nottingham*. Her two lifeboats were demolished, and the ship, now exposed and helpless, was in danger of breaking apart. Three of her threatened crew offered to take the ship's yawl and attempt to make shore to summon help.

Watchman John Karp, oiler William Best, and deck-hand J. F. Thornburn gently lowered the tiny boat into the tempest, but it almost immediately smashed against the side of the ship, throwing the three hapless crewmen into the roiling water where they disappeared.

It would be several days before the weather moderated sufficiently to send wrecking tugs to jettison the wheat and refloat the ship. The surviving crew members—fourteen men and a female cook—were taken off.

In spite of the fury expended by the storm of November 1913, a surprising number of ships on Superior during those terrifying days managed to limp into safe harbor, showing heavy damage in some instances and a ponderous covering of ice but still afloat. One such ship was the battered and bruised passenger steamer *Huronic*, which made Whitefish Bay and beached herself on a sandbar where it waited for the storm to blow herself out before being refloated by tugs.

Unfortunately, the drowned men of the *Nottingham* would not be the only fatalities experienced in the worst blow ever to hit the Great Lakes.

CHAPTER 5

The Unlucky Skipper
and the Jonah Boat

MANY A LAKESIDE VILLAGE OR TOWN HAD a very personal
connection with the disasters that from time to time occurred on the lakes. The crews of the ships operating over
these waters frequently settled in communities abutting
the water, marrying and raising their families while sailing
away during the shipping season, returning to their loved
ones during the winter months when nothing moved on
the frozen waters. But too often they didn't come home at
all, and when a steamer was dragged to the bottom of one
of the lakes, an entire town could be affected and sent into
bitter mourning at the loss.

Half of the eighteen-man crew of the Algoma Central
Steamship Company's *Leafield* was from Collingwood,
Ontario, a small village on Nottawasaga Bay in Lake
Huron.

Captain Charles Baker had hired Captain Alfred
Northcott as his first mate, Fred Begley as second mate,
and Eddie Whitesides as one of his wheelsmen. He also
selected Paul and Richard Shefield as stewards.

The Shefields were an irrepressible pair who, while
ashore, fought like panthers over just about anything in
their lives, from a local barmaid they had both taken a
fancy to to whether Canadian ale was more robust and
satisfying than Canadian lager.

37

"It was nothing to see them come crashing out of the front door of McKinley's Hotel [tavern], kicking, biting, punching one another, both bloody as slaughtered sows and both actin' like their fondest wish was to kill the other," a family friend recalled later. "On the other hand, the disagreements rarely lasted more than a couple of rounds and never amounted to much more than a bloody nose or a black eye, a swollen lip or, maybe, a lost tooth. And no one had better have anything unkind to say about the other or, be-jesus, there would be a riot for sure."

"There was no question that Pauly and Dick fought a lot," a relative would later state. "They had since they were little kids and one tried to take the other's toy. The same when they grew up and began to fancy the girls. Dick couldn't resist trying to take a lass away from Paul no matter he'd not the slightest interest in her himself. But they truly loved one another . . . they truly did."

"They were just fine when they reported back for work," a former shipmate remembered. "They'd come crawling up the gangway, all sloshed from a night on the town, their arms around each other and their faces looking like they'd been pushed into an electric fan. But by the time they went on watch, they'd be all cleaned up, sober as judges and all business. But just wait until we hit the next port."

As was the custom of the times, the ship's chief engineer chose his assistants as well as the engine room "black gang." Andy Kerr, the *Leafield's* chief engineer, had hired Tom Bowie as his first assistant and Charlie Brown as one of the firemen. All were from Collingwood, as were Leo Doyle, an oiler aboard the steamer *Regina*, wheelsman Joseph Simpson, and Ernest Hughes, a fireman on the *James C. Carruthers.*

The 227-foot *Leafield* was one of three well-deck freighters built in England as saltwater tramp, or coaster, vessels that were brought to the Great Lakes for ore and grain operations between the Algoma Steel Corporation mill at the Canadian Soo and the furnaces of the Canada Iron Corporation at Midland, Ontario. Frequently during the shipping season the *Leafield* loaded grain at Fort William, Ontario, and coal at Toledo, Ohio. She also carried steel railroad rails on her deck.

The *Leafield* was considered an unlucky boat by some mariners familiar with the vessel's past. The previous season she had run on a shoal in Georgian Bay and tore her bottom out, putting her out of commission for two months and costing her owners a small fortune in salvage and repair costs. Her master at the time was Andrew "Sandy" McIntyre, and company officials felt that he had been guilty of gross carelessness resulting in the wreck. He was transferred at the beginning of the 1913 season to another boat.

Whether McIntyre was as blundering as some believed or simply the victim of a star-crossed company—as others argued—would be a matter of contention long after the 1913 season was over.

The ships of the Algoma Central Steamship Company fleet seemed to have a predisposition for disaster. The *Monkshaven*, upbound with a load of railroad rails in November of 1905, ran on the rocks and sank at Pie Island in Thunder Bay. A year later—also in November—the *Theano*, also carrying railroad rails, went down after hitting a reef at Trowbridge Island. Now it was again November and word came into Port Arthur that the *Leafield* had gone missing.

The battered cruise liner *Huronic* limped into the Soo heavily laden with ice, her pilothouse demolished, her master nearly frozen to death, and her passengers emotional cripples after more than forty-eight hours of terror. One of Captain Cameron's first acts after docking was to report having seen a vessel he believed to be the *Leafield* on the rocks of Angus Island not far from the spot on Pie Island where the derelict *Monkshaven* still lay awash.

Later, a second reported sighting came from Captain W. C. Jordon of the steamer *Franz*. Jordon was the brother-in-law of Fred Begley, the *Leafield*'s second mate. He said that the *Leafield* had been ahead of him when the gale struck, and then driving snow had blocked further sightings of the boat. When the *Franz* arrived at Fort William, Jordon inquired about the *Leafield* and was told that the ship had not arrived.

A tug was later dispatched to Angus Island but it found nothing. The water at the location where Captain Cameron had seen the *Leafield* was 155 fathoms deep. The ship had piled on the rocks, had her hull ripped out, and was then pulled by the wind and waves back into the water, where she went down with all eighteen members of her crew.

A piece of broken uppermast without identifying marks was found and brought to Fort William. By chance, Sandy McIntyre, now skippering the *Thomas J. Drummond*, was in port and was shown the piece of mast.

"I can definitely state," said McIntyre, "that this is not part of the vessel *Leafield*."

No wreckage from the *Leafield* was ever recovered.

The icy cold of the Big Lake tends to halt the natural formation of gasses in the human bodies submerged in it, gasses that are normally responsible for a dead body eventually floating to the surface. Thus has developed a sailor's axiom: "Lake Superior never gives up her dead."

No bodies from the *Leafield* were ever found.

CHAPTER 6

"Wire the Owners That I'm Coming"

THE 1913 SHIPPING SEASON ON THE GREAT LAKES was for Captain Jimmy Owen extraordinary in two respects: it marked his thirty-sixth year on the lakes, and it was also his seventh as master of the 525-foot ore carrier *Henry B. Smith*. The year 1913 was significant for the fifty-four-year-old mariner for another, less splendid accomplishment. The season had been the most calamitous nine months of his life. "Jimmy Bad-luck" was a mirthful sobriquet that had made the rounds of docks and waterfront saloons of many ports of call visited by the *Smith*.

Owen had mastered the Acme Transit Company's flagship since her launching at Lorain, Ohio, on May 2, 1906, as hull number 343. Insured with Lloyd's of London for $338,000—a princely sum at the turn of the century—she was one of the largest freighters on the Great Lakes.

Jimmy had been considered as the favored shipmaster by the Cleveland, Ohio, shipping company owned by William A. and Arthur Harrison Hawgood, a lake shipping family that boasted no less than eight freighters. The fact that the *Smith* had never known a master other than Jimmy Owen attested to the firm's confidence and admiration for the brusque, blunt, and outspoken man with the sinless countenance of a Kentucky bible thumper.

"It has been said of many men that they were generous to a fault," someone once remarked in describing James L. Owen. "Somebody may invent a better phrase some day, but that accurately describes Captain Owen. Nobody with a worthy cause ever appealed to him for financial aid in vain."

As one of the oldest shipmasters on the lakes, he was considered by his peers as among the most able and dependable of mariners; his ships consistently fulfilled the quotas set by the Hawgoods, whose family crest might well have borne the motto "Bring your cargo in on time."

But almost from the beginning of the 1913 season, Jimmy's performance had been less than satisfactory. He—and his vessel—were mysteriously clouded by an unexplainable series of misfortunes. He frequently was plagued by poor scheduling which brought his boat into port only to discover that a number of other vessels were there ahead of him, occupying the loading or unloading docks and thereby causing several days' delay in his departure. On other occasions he found himself in constricted passages enveloped in fog, making it necessary to wait at anchor for hours for the weather to clear. Mechanical breakdowns in dock equipment happened with frightening regularity during the 1913 season. Errors in loading orders that took time to correct; delays caused by injuries to vital crew members; the failure in one port for the chandler to arrive to resupply the boat with necessary food items cost more than half a day's steaming time.

None of the problems were directly attributable to the redoubtable captain. But the Hawgoods, frustrated with the seemingly endless tardiness of cargo deliveries and pickups, began to question their top skipper's performance; he was roundly chastised as the season wore on and, by November, word from Cleveland gave Jimmy the unmistakable understanding that he had better produce if he expected to command an Acme Transit Company boat in 1914.

Decidedly worried when the *Henry B. Smith* arrived in Marquette, Michigan, from Milwaukee on Friday morning, November 7, Jimmy was pleased to find his boat under the loading chutes at the Duluth South Shore & Atlantic Railroad dock Friday evening. He gleefully anticipated being out of the harbor early Saturday, which would guarantee him an on-time delivery for this trip and perhaps silence some of the growling that had been coming from the Perry Payne Building headquarters of the Acme Transit Company.

But in keeping with the insidious problems that had haunted him throughout the season, the iron ore in the railroad hopper cars froze together, refusing to move easily and slowing the loading process to a crawl. Fires that were lit beneath the hopper cars in an effort to thaw them out met with little success. Jimmy smoldered through the night—some said he went to a saloon and got so drunk he had to be helped back aboard his ship by a pair of burly dockworkers.

The storm struck on Saturday morning, and to his horror, Jimmy learned that the loading-dock crews had been sent home with his ship still half-loaded. They were not scheduled to return until Monday morning. He appealed to dock officials, who were aware of the shipowner's dissatisfaction with Captain Owen, and, in a demonstration of pity, took the unusual step of ordering the crews to complete loading the *Smith* Sunday morning.

An extra day's delay did little to mitigate Jimmy's apprehension over his employers' almost certain ire at yet another late arrival by the *Henry B. Smith*. Still, it was better than being two days behind schedule.

As if the fretful captain hadn't enough to worry about, Sunday afternoon, as the loading was nearing completion, his second mate, James Burke—who had been suffering with a severe chest cold that he felt was turning to pneumonia—informed Jimmy that he was calling it quits for the season and was catching a train for the Soo, where he could make connections that would take him home to Cleveland. And deckhand Edward Whalen also announced that he was leaving the boat there at Marquette, giving no reason for his departure.

One member of the crew who stayed was twenty-year-old porter Lawrence Perry of Duluth, Minnesota.

Perry, who had begun working on the lakes in the spring of 1912, had joined the *Smith* six weeks earlier. He was the son of Louis Perry of Duluth and was one of twenty-four children, ten of whom were still living. Lawrence had urged his brother George to work the lake boats with him, but George said the water had not much attraction for him and declined.

During the day on Sunday, Jimmy visited the dock office and announced that he would sail as soon as the loading had been completed. "Please wire the owners that I am coming."

Late Sunday afternoon, as soon as the last ore pocket had been loaded aboard, Captain Owen signaled to the surprised dockworkers to cast off his boat. By this time the storm was raging and the *Smith*'s thirty-two hatches had not been covered. It was a job that normally took several hours.

As the equally dumbfounded deck crew scurried frantically to secure the hatch covers, tarpaulins, and locking bars and clamps, the *Henry B. Smith* slowly backed away from the dock and swung her bow toward the harbor breakwater, obviously intending to sail out into the worst November storm in memory.

Captain Charles Fox watched with disbelief from the bridge of his boat, the *Choctaw*, as the *Smith* steamed out of the harbor to be immediately assaulted by the towering waves that washed over her bow, above her pilothouse, and cascaded down upon the wretched deckhands desperately trying to close the hatches.

It took but a few terror-filled minutes for Jimmy Owen to realize that he had made a tragic mistake in thinking he could sail straight into the lake. Instead of turning to starboard on a course that would take him directly to the Soo, he ordered his boat swung to port to steer for the shelter of Keweenaw Point, where several other vessels were already anchored. The boat rolled frighteningly in the troughs of the seas before disappearing from the view of the appalled witnesses.

Three days later, Dan Johnson, walking along the beach near Marquette, spotted bits and pieces of wreckage that had washed ashore. There were cabin doors and white-painted pieces of wood, one of which had the name *Henry B. Smith* lettered on it. There were four oars and a pike pole. Three of the oars were stenciled *Henry B. Smith*. The hapless Jimmy Owen, the *Henry B. Smith*, and her twenty-three-man crew never reached the safety of Keweenaw Point.

In Marquette, Mr. and Mrs. F. O. Brown of Cleveland breathed a sigh of relief and wondered what mysterious force had intervened to save their lives. Close friends of Jimmy Owen, they had planned to sail home with the *Smith* after having visited friends in Marquette. But for some unexplained reason, Jimmy had not notified them of his departure.

It was several days before word reached Cleveland of the loss of the *Smith* and all her crew. It was several more days before James Burke managed to arrive home. In the meantime, the newspapers had published the names of the drowned crew members, including Burke's and that of Edward Whalen. The Acme Transit Company, which supplied the list, was unaware that the two men had departed the boat in Marquette.

CHAPTER 7

"I'll Tell Your Father We Passed You"

THE STORM BATTERED LAKE SUPERIOR THE SEVENTH, eighth, and ninth of November 1913, extracting a terrible toll from the vessels caught in its path.

The *Leafield* and *Henry B. Smith* had gone down with all hands; the *L. C. Waldo*, *Turret Chief*, and *Major* had been thrown on the rocks and were total losses; the *William Nottingham* was wrecked near Duluth but salvageable, as were the steamers *F. G. Hartwell* and *J. T. Hutchinson* in Whitefish Bay; an uncounted number received damage in varying degrees of severity; and all who made port did so bearing a thick coat of thousands of tons of ice. Forty-one men had drowned.

By Sunday night, the storm seemed to be losing its punch and many mariners expected little further difficulty negotiating any of the lakes—at least for the next several days. Great Lakes storms rarely followed one close behind the other.

Those auditing the awful carnage resulting from the storm could little imagine that the worst was still to come, and within hours.

Three boats that had made it through the Lake Superior hurricane locked down at the Soo early Saturday evening: the *J. H. Sheadle*, under the command of Captain S. A. Lyons, the *James C. Carruthers*, commanded by Captain William H. Wright, and the *Hydrus*, skippered by Captain John H. Lowe.

Owned by the St. Lawrence & Chicago Steam Navigation Company of Toronto, the 529-foot *Carruthers* was not yet six months old, a spanking new steel-hulled freighter with a gross tonnage of 7,862 tons. Built in Collingwood, Ontario, as hull number 38 by the Collingwood Shipbuilding Company, she was launched on May 22, 1913.

Having spent most of the season in fitting out and in sea trials, the *Carruthers* was on her third trip, with 375,000 bushels of wheat loaded at Fort William, Ontario.

As the three boats slowly negotiated the narrow, winding lower St. Marys River headed south from the Soo Locks to Lake Huron, the *Carruthers* was in the lead followed by the *Sheadle*—also loaded with wheat from Fort William—and the *Hydrus*, heavy with iron ore. The *Carruthers* met the upbound freighter *Midland Prince*. Angus "Ray" McMillan, the *Carruthers*'s wheelsman, spotted a familiar figure leaning against the upbound ship's after deckhouse. It was Jack Daley, a close friend from the Canadian port of Midland on Georgian Bay.

McMillan shouted across the short distance separating the two boats, "We're going to Midland this time, Jack. I'll tell your father we passed you." The *Midland Prince*'s fireman waved and disappeared into the deckhouse.

Daley would make it to Midland later; McMillan would not. Two of the three vessels in the small convoy would disappear beneath Lake Huron waters without a trace.

PART II
LAKE MICHIGAN

CHAPTER 8

"Might See You in Heaven"

BECAUSE OF ITS LENGTH—ALMOST 350 unbroken miles—
Lake Michigan often is the most tempestuous of the Great
Lakes. When the wind is out of the north, huge waves can
pile up, gaining speed and power as they sweep down the
long stretch from Michigan's Upper Peninsula to the shores
of Indiana and Illinois. In a strong wind, the water depths
near Chicago have been known to rise by almost ten feet.
Lake Michigan, along with Lake Huron, lays claim to the
greatest toll over the years of ships taken in Great Lakes
storms.

Saturday, November 8, 1913, began as an unusually
serene autumn day. A number of commercial vessels were
plying Lake Michigan waters, going about their tasks unaware that the phlegmatic character of the weather was
about to make a frightening change to the bellicose.

Built seven years before the start of the American
Civil War as a 225-foot two-masted schooner, the *Plymouth*, her masts cut off and her canvas removed, had
been relegated to functioning as a powerless barge, trans-
porting lumber and potatoes from Illinois, Wisconsin, and
Michigan ports for McKinnon & Scott of Menominee,
Michigan. Her captain, Axel Larsen, was a cautious and
capable seaman of many years' experience, but the six
others in the crew were severely lacking in training or

51

experience. One of these was Deputy United States Marshal Chris Keenan, a young, handsome non-sailor who had been assigned to the *Plymouth* as a custodian of the barge pending settlement in federal court between the owners and lumber companies attempting to collect claimed debts. Keenan's responsibility aboard was to insure that no harm was done to the vessel until the scheduled April court date could determine rightful ownership.

The *Plymouth*'s directional power came from the *James H. Martin*, a forty-four-year-old tug that had seen its better days on the lakes. Making his first trip aboard the tug was Captain Louis Setunsky, a seasoned veteran of the lakes who apparently suffered from a careless choice of commands. He discovered almost immediately that the *Martin* was not what she had been represented to be; she tended to leak like a sieve in anything livelier than a dead calm. And if that wasn't enough, the antiquated tug was grossly underpowered.

On the other hand, Donald McKinnon, the tug's engineer, believed the vessel to be suitably seaworthy for her assigned task. In his opinion, she was watertight and acceptably powered. Of course, in addition to acting as the *Martin*'s engineer, McKinnon was one of the tug's owners.

On Friday, November 7, the *Martin* with the *Plymouth* in tow cleared the Menominee light, bound for Lake Huron with a load of lumber. The storm warnings were posted just two hours after their departure and neither the captain nor crew were aware that they were sailing into the worst storm to strike Lake Michigan in memory.

Also out in the lake unaware and unprepared was the steamer *Louisiana*, a twenty-six-year-old wooden-hulled freighter bound for Escanaba, on the western shore of the lake, for a load of iron ore after making a delivery of coal at Milwaukee.

Ahead of the *Louisiana*, steaming up Little Bay de

Noc, on her way to Gladstone, Michigan, was the steamer *James H. Prentice* with the barge *Halstead* under tow. Like the *Plymouth*, the *Halstead* had once been a trim and beautiful 170-foot schooner that had fallen on hard times and was now relegated to hauling lumber.

The brisk southerly wind that had followed the vessels throughout Saturday night suddenly ceased, then puffed several times and was gone. At 12:15 A.M. Sunday, the wind came raging out of the northwest without warning and within thirty minutes had grown to a fifty-five-mile-an-hour gale.

The *Louisiana* without cargo found herself unable to make headway in the fierce winds and rising seas. The anchors were dropped in the hope it would keep the boat from being driven backward. But even with the engines running at full speed ahead, the wind was winning the battle. By 1:00 A.M. the winds had increased to seventy miles an hour and a full-blown blizzard was assaulting the vessel with snow and ice.

Captain Fred McDonald decided that the better part of valor was to give up the futile attempt and to haul around and run for safety. The nearest haven was Washington Harbor, on the northwest finger of Washington Island.

Now the *Louisiana* faced a brand new peril: the wind and waves were driving them ever closer to the beach and they were powerless to prevent it. At 2:00 A.M. the boat ground ashore. They were now at the mercy of the waves, which pounded the craft with a relentless determination to batter it to pieces.

It took six hours to get a man ashore to take the news of the wreck to the nearest lifesaving station.

While the exhausted and cold crew waited for rescue, yet a new threat to their lives appeared.

"How it happened we never knew for certain, but the old *Louisiana* caught fire," First Mate Finley McLean recalled later. "The old craft was made of wood and burned like tinder."

Fighting the fire was hopeless. Frantically, they managed to launch one of the lifeboats and the entire crew of twenty scrambled aboard to battle the huge breakers to reach the shore. Half-drowned, nearly frozen, and paralyzed with fear, the crew watched the entire ship become engulfed in flames.

"She burned clear to the water as we watched," McLean remembered. "There was nothing left of her but red-hot engines, which hissed like a volcano and sent off clouds of steam as the seas rushed over them."

They abandoned the smoking hulk of the *Louisiana* to seek shelter from the murderous blizzard that was escalating by the minute. The nearest house was five miles away—five miles of snowdrifts, many of which were over their heads. Some method of getting through the drifts had to be devised.

"Since I was the smallest man in the crew, they chose me for the trail-breaker," McLean stated later. "The big men would pick me up, then after a good swing would throw me against a snow bank, and crawl in after me. I didn't like this chilly trick any too well, you can bet."

However, the novel approach was effective, and the crew was able to make its way to a farmhouse where they were given dry clothes, food, and the chance to thaw out.

McLean was anxious to notify his wife that he was alive and well in the event that she would hear of the wreck and worry about his safety.

He fought his way to the nearest telegraph station, where he managed to get a message started. The telegrapher began tapping out McLean's message but all that got through was : "LOUISIANA WRECKED ON WASHINGTON ISLAND . . . " At this crucial point the telegraph wires went down. Fortunately, the operator on the receiving end guessed the purpose of the message and added the word "SAVED."

In the meantime, the crewman sent for help found his way to the nearby Plum Island Life Saving Station. The lifesavers rushed to the *Louisiana* only to discover that the vessel had been destroyed by fire and that the crew was safe. Still, their dash to the stricken boat turned out not to be a fool's errand. They were needed nearby.

In Washington Harbor were several other vessels. The *J. M. Stevens* and *Minerva* struggled against mountainous seas. Their anchors were holding and the boats seemed to be winning the contest. This was not the case, however, with the barge *Halstead*.

The towline connecting it to the *Prentice* parted and the barge was driven into Washington Harbor, her anchors dragging the bottom, distress signals flying.

The *Halstead* and her seven-man crew were thrown on the rocks a short distance from the smoldering remnants of the *Louisiana*.

The lifesavers rushed to get as close to the endangered vessel as the waves would allow, hoping to fire a line to her and to send a breeches buoy to the men aboard. But a powerful wave struck the barge, picking her up and carrying her over the reef and onto the beach, where the crew could easily scramble ashore.

The second barge in the area did not fare so well.

Less than ten miles to the northeast, in the lee of St. Martin Island, the tug *James H. Martin* was preparing to move back into Lake Michigan. Captain Setunsky had sought refuge there when his underpowered craft began having difficulties towing the barge *Plymouth*. With the southwest winds quartering on the stern, the barge continually skewed to one side or the other, putting the tug in danger of capsizing.

When the winds swung to the northwest and then north, Setunsky decided the creaky old tug would only be able to make headway without the annoying swinging of the barge. Within a mile of St. Martin Island, the captain realized that he had overestimated the tug's capabilities. Now desperate, Setunsky came to a fateful decision: he would leave the *Plymouth* at anchor in the lee of tiny Gull Island and beat a hasty retreat, alone, to the safety of St. Martin Island to await the end of the blow.

The tug signaled the barge to drop anchor and let go the tow line. As they watched, helpless, the crew of the barge saw the *Martin* steam slowly away, frequently hidden from view in the deep troughs of the towering waves. They had been abandoned to the vagaries of the savage storm. The fact that the actions of Captain Setunsky were considered appropriate and prudent under the circumstances did little to comfort the men in the barge or disabuse them of the notion that they had been offered to the storm gods as a sacrifice to insure the survival of the *Martin* and her crew.

The north wind howling down the lake brought with it a steadily falling thermometer and heavy snows.

Nearly sixty hours later, Captain Setunsky became convinced that the storm had sufficiently blown itself out and he could now proceed back into the lake to retrieve his consort. But when they reached Gull Island, the *Plymouth* was nowhere to be seen. She was *gone!*

Residents of Menominee—the barge's home port— were incensed; it was a widespread belief that the captain of the *Martin* had marooned the helpless men of the *Plymouth* without making even a small attempt at taking them off the doomed barge. The public rage increased a week later when a bottle washed ashore near Pentwater, Michigan—on the opposite side of Lake Michigan. Inside the bottle was a poignant note from Chris Keenan which indicated that the owner, McKinnon, had callously and cruelly deserted the seven men of the *Plymouth* in a cowardly act to save his own life.

Captain Setunsky defended his actions, stating, "A rescue was out of the question." Owner Donald McKinnon argued that the tug was taking water badly and was in no condition to aid the barge. He dismissed Keenan's note as "the fancy of an insane man."

A few days later, the body of the deputy U.S. marshal was found on the beach about ten miles north of Manistee, more than eighty miles from Gull Island. Almost a month later, Captain Larsen reached the shore for the last time eighty miles south of where Keenan was found and one hundred and twenty miles from where the *Plymouth* had been left. The wrecked barge, Clifford Duchaine, Clyde Jessup, Peter Johnson, James Sabota, and Henry Kossak—the other members of the *Plymouth* crew—were never found.

As public indignation over the incident rose, the two principals began to argue about their original statements concerning the loss of the *Plymouth*. McKinnon publicly accused Captain Setunsky of "incompetency and unseamanlike handling of the tug during the storm," while Setunsky declared that the condition of the vessel and its machinery was misrepresented to him by McKinnon who, he asserted, "gave me to understand that everything was in apple-pie order and there was no reason to doubt the statement of the licensed engineer of the boat."

An investigation into the seaworthiness of the battered tug quickly became academic. On November 30, the *James H. Martin* sank to the bottom of the Menominee harbor.

The note found in the bottle was delivered to Keenan's family. It read:

> Dear wife and children. We were left up here
> in Lake Michigan by McKinnon, captain (of the)

James H. Martin, tug at anchor. He went away
and never said goodbye or anything to us. Lost
one man yesterday. We have been out in storm
forty hours. Goodbye dear ones, I might see you
in Heaven.

Pray for me. Chris K.

P.S. I felt so bad I had another man write for
me.

Goodbye forever.

CHAPTER 9

The Weather Ashore

THE STORM THAT THRASHED ACROSS THE GREAT LAKES for five days in November caused considerable havoc ashore in parts of Wisconsin, Illinois, and Michigan, and much of Indiana, Ohio, and Pennsylvania.

In Milwaukee, hundreds of citizens turned out in bitter cold and strong north winds to watch fifteen hundred feet of a new municipal breakwater project be systematically destroyed by the tremendous seas. Two floating pile drivers were also wrecked.

In Muskegon, Michigan, where the winds were reported to be eighty miles an hour, several factory smokestacks were blown down, store windows were blown in, tops of houses were lifted and carried away, and signs, fences, pieces of roofing, and other debris filled the air.

More than $150,000 in damage was done to the docks and landfill along the Chicago lakefront. Here too the spectacle of Mother Nature at her most furious worst drew thousands to the lakefront on Sunday in spite of the terrible wind and cold. Two men were literally picked up by the gale and thrown to their deaths in the Chicago River.

Water flooded Lake Shore Drive, surrounded the Convent of La Rabida and the German Building in the Lincoln Park neighborhood, swept over a twelve-foot pier in Lin-

59

coln Park, and threatened to damage the Illinois Central Railroad tracks. Numerous electric wires were blown down in the storm.

Also in Lincoln Park, millions of dollars worth of newly created landfill was washed out into Lake Michigan. William Neilson, superintendent of the park, estimated that it would cost an additional $100,000 to replace the several thousand cubic yards of soil that had been lost.

Among the awestruck citizens watching the destruction of the Lincoln Park extension was Daniel F. Rice, chairman of the park extension committee. It was said that Rice audibly groaned as each wave struck and dragged great chunks of earth away.

The *Chicago Tribune* stated: "It was the biggest job of groaning he has done in years."

All up and down Lake Michigan the scene was the same as docks and piers disappeared and hundreds of pleasure craft were demolished. Buildings of every type were damaged or destroyed and the injuries were uncountable. The lone godsend was the absence of heavy snow to drift and clog roads and highways.

Other cities farther east were not so fortunate.

In Detroit, it began shortly before noon on Sunday, November 9. The wind, which from seven that morning had been from the north at eighteen miles an hour, suddenly began to increase, building in strength until by two in the afternoon a full-blown gale was lashing the city. The snow, which had been falling since noon, swirled in the high winds and began to drift. Only the most hardy braved the outdoors and many pedestrians caught outside were picked up and driven to shelters by taxis and streetcars.

The barometer was at 28.35, the lowest barometric pressure ever recorded at the Detroit station. The temperature at daybreak had been fifty degrees Fahrenheit. By nine that morning the thermometer was reading twenty-nine degrees, finally leveling off at twenty-two degrees about 9:00 P.M. It would fall another ten degrees the following day.

A number of injuries caused by the high winds and blowing snow were reported throughout the city. Lobby front windows exploded in at several hotels in the downtown section of the city. Falling glass and stone caused a number of minor injuries as did several accidents between streetcars and taxicabs unable to see one another in the blinding blizzard. Telephone and telegraph services were severely curtailed due to the many downed wires and poles.

In Toledo the temperature registered twenty-two degrees at seven o'clock Monday morning, and snow depths were reported at between four and five inches on the level with deep drifts throughout the city. Five gangs of twenty-five men each were mustered to clear the main streets, while sixteen teams of horses were hitched to dump wagons to cart the snow away.

Electric service was interrupted in many parts of the city and a strike of Rail-Light linemen prevented speedy restoration of service. Schools and many downtown businesses were closed on Monday.

As bad as it seemed to most Toledoans, the storm failed to halt two determined thieves.

Within a short span of twenty minutes, a pair of Toledo beat patrolmen arrested two men in the act of mugging pedestrians in the downtown business district. In both cases the victim had been battered to the ground and his pockets rifled. In the first instance the two cops arrived just as the mugger was leaving the scene with a wallet containing $5.50 taken from an out-of-town salesman. In the second, the mugger was nabbed in the act of going through the pockets of the prostrate "muggee."

The gale-driven blizzard struck all along the Lake Huron and Lake Erie shores. Duck hunters, lured onto the lakes by the mild temperatures prior to Saturday, found themselves in extreme peril, and several were reported missing when small rowboats and skiffs were found bearing coats and other personal effects but no bodies.

Two men were drowned when they attempted to sail a twenty-four-foot boat across an eight-mile stretch of Lake St. Clair, heading for an island they never reached.

Many small communities were isolated in northern Ohio and Ontario as deep snow drifts blocked roads and rail lines and communication wires were knocked down.

Near Sarnia, Ontario, three train crewmen were killed when the caboose of the train they were manning was struck from behind by a second train unable to see them in the driving snow.

A ten-inch snowfall in Pittsburgh was blown into four-foot drifts by a forty-mile-an-hour wind. Almost twelve inches of snow fell in Canton, paralyzing the city. Dayton was largely spared damage and severe disruption when a modest one to three inches of snow fell there, but fifteen-foot drifts were reported in Upper Sandusky, Ohio.

Even the replicas of Columbus's ships that had been touring the lakes were not spared the storm. The *Santa Maria* was torn from its moorings in Erie Harbor, where the three ships were wintering, and thrown onto a sandbar outside the harbor. Tugs labored throughout the day on November 10, trying to free the caravel without success. It was feared that all efforts to save her would be fruitless.

A wide band of snow and wind stretched from Duluth southeast as far as West Virginia, and freezing or near freezing temperatures were found in northern Florida.

By far the hardest-hit city was Cleveland.

The storm deposited twenty-four inches of snow on the city that the strong winds quickly whipped into drifts as high as five feet. Light poles and wires littered the streets, the poles snapped by the wind and the wires pulled down from the weight of the snow. The community was almost completely cut off from the outside world. Supplies of bread, meat, and vegetables practically halted, and milk was rationed only to those who had infants or small children. The situation became so grave that city officials feared a wide-spread famine unless roads were opened soon.

The dead in the city, in hospitals, funeral establishments, and other facilities, were forced to remain where they were, awaiting the opening of the roads and the clearing of cemeteries.

Five men were killed in Cleveland during the storm: one electrocuted by a downed power wire, another killed when he fell from a moving boxcar, a third when a portion of the roof on his house collapsed on him, a fourth burned to death in a fire, and the fifth was found dead in a snowbank, possibly, it was believed, of a heart attack.

Telephone and telegraph communication with other cities was cut off, and electric power was off for a large portion of the city as storm-damaged power stations broke down.

To the east, from Cleveland to the Pennsylvania line and beyond, and to the west from Cleveland to Toledo, numerous trains were trapped in snowbanks, the passengers struggling to keep from freezing to death.

Drinking water from churned-up Lake Erie had to be boiled before using.

After battling a large fire in the manufacturing section that resulted in $75,000 in damage, the fire department expressed doubt it would be able to fight another blaze of that size in the high winds being experienced.

The blizzard was the worst early-November snowstorm in Cleveland's history. It would be days before essential services could be restored, weeks before daily routine in the city would be back to normal, and months before all the damage was fully repaired. And for those who lived through it, the great storm of 1913 would linger in their memories for a lifetime.

PART III
DEADLY HURON

CHAPTER 10

Dancing Chauncey's Last Waltz

THE PAIR OF WEATHER SYSTEMS THAT HAD SPED to Lake Superior from the west to unite in the catastrophic gale of November seventh, eighth, and ninth now churned south, into Lake Huron. Picking up moisture and heat from the lower lake, the storm grew in strength as it rushed down from Sault Ste. Marie, catching a number of boats unprepared.

Shipmasters who had suffered the storm's wrath on Superior turned a deaf ear to the continued storm warnings flying at weather stations and wrongly assumed that the gale had blown itself out, that it was now safe to proceed south with their cargoes.

At the other end of the lakes, weather forecasts were ignored with equal cynicism, boat captains preferring to trust in their own judgment and their past experience with November storms.

One such commander was Captain Chauncey R. Nye, master of the 432-foot bulk carrier *John A. McGean.*

Nye was a jaunty, fun-loving mariner with twenty-seven years' service on the lakes. He'd lived in Detroit ten years earlier, serving as pilot of the Detroit fireboat *James Battle.* Later, he joined the Cleveland Cliffs Iron Company as master of the steamer *Pioneer.* He also commanded the steamers *Pontiac* and *Angeline,* the *George B. Leonard* and *Charles Hubbard* of the United States Transportation Company, and the *John Stanton* and *John A. McGean* for Hutchinson and Company.

Well liked in almost every port on the lakes, he was known as "Dancing Chauncey" because of his fondness for "tripping the light fantastic." Dancing was Chauncey's passion and he grumbled mightily when his duties required that he be at sea on Fridays and Saturdays, his traditional nights to howl.

Nye's wife, Eve, was an understanding woman who suffered Chauncey's ballroom addiction with quiet patience, just as she did his annual failure to be home for their wedding anniversary. As she did each year, she inquired of Chauncey before he left on November 8 for a trip up the lakes if he would be home on December 16.

"When I asked my husband if he would be here on that day, he jested like he always did about my 'solitary dinner,' for he never returned before Christmas. 'Have a nice anniversary dinner and play I am sitting opposite,' he said."

The *McGean* sailed with a load of coal and a crew of twenty-three, bound for Superior. At 2:10 Sunday morning she cleared Port Huron and headed out into Lake Huron with fresh northwest winds on her bow. A few minutes behind her was the steamer *Isaac M. Scott*, also headed north.

The two vessels hugged the western lakeshore to take advantage of the protective effect of the landmass, which tended to blunt the force of winds screaming across it.

The steel freighter was considered a very seaworthy craft. Five years old, the boat was relatively new, having been built at the A. M. Shipbuilders Company yards in Lorain, Ohio, as hull number 359. Owned by the Pioneer Steamship Company and managed by Hutchinson and Company, she was launched February 22, 1908. Captain

Nye was completing his second shipping season aboard the vessel.

On board the boat, serving as wheelsmen, were two men from the Sarnia, Ontario, area. George Smith and Thomas Stone were full-blooded North American Indians, members of the Seneca and Ojibwa tribes whose people lived on reservations in southern Ontario.

The *McGean* proceeded up the lake with Captain Nye on the bridge observing the mounting waves, the winds screeching in the rigging, and the hull of the boat pounding in the seas, sounding much like cannon shots each time the bow raised and crashed down again. He was totally unaware that Mother Nature was stirring up a potent brew, the likes of which few shipmasters on the Great Lakes had ever seen and survived.

On the "DeTour Track," an imaginary line that would take the freighter on a straight-line course from Lake Huron to the port of DeTour, Michigan, south of the St. Marys River and ultimately to the Soo Locks, the *McGean* was far out in the middle of the lake about fourteen miles north of Tawas Point.

Now, without the shelter of the western coastline of the lake, the boat was at the mercy of the wind and waves. The winds were registering out of the northwest at fifty-five miles an hour on the boat's anemometer, strong but not so bad as to cause undue concern on the part of the seasoned captain.

And then, with little or no warning, the gale began to quarter, swinging to the north, then the northeast, the east, and finally coming from the south. How could that be? Chauncey wondered. The seas, too, were behaving in an outrageous fashion, striking the sides of the vessel first on the port then the starboard, first on the bow then from astern.

As he stood in the pilothouse looking out at the

raging foam the captain might well have thought that he had never seen anything to resemble this madness. He would have been right.

The storm system born out of two weather cells coming from the west had been joined by an extremely rare third system rushing up through Georgia from the Gulf of Mexico. It brought with it a terrible energy, the result of superheated moisture drawn up from the warm waters of the Caribbean, fuel to feed itself and the storm awaiting it over Lake Huron. It was like bringing gasoline to throw on a fire already burning out of control. It would cause Lake Huron to behave in a deadly fashion, the like of which had never been experienced in the living memory of man.

This aberration of a storm would be responsible for the greatest loss of life in a single storm on any of the Great Lakes. It would take freighters such as the *McGean* and twist and tear them and batter them into scrap metal before tossing them on the rocks along the shore, or it would rend their hulls, open them to the roaring torrent, flood them beyond their power to maintain buoyancy, and then it would suck them and their terrified crews to the bottom.

At a point about ten miles off Kettle Point, something happened to cause the *McGean*'s rudder to be partially torn from its skeg. It's not known whether the damage resulted from a wave striking it or if the boat struck some object in the water. Whatever it was, the loose rudder smashed into the propeller, breaking off one of its blades.

The loss of one "bucket" would have caused the boat to shake terribly and the disconnected rudder would have left the *McGean* helpless and out of control in the viciously writhing seas. It would have taken only minutes for the boat to be swung broadside to the waves and pulled into a deep valley, unable to prevent an onrushing mountain of water from completely overwhelming the craft.

When the killer wave struck, the windows in the pilot-house crashed in on Chauncey and his wheelsman. The pilothouse walls began to buckle and tear apart. The sky-lights over the engine room were blasted in and the lake poured inside. Thousands of tons of water smashed down on the *McGean* like a gigantic fist to crush the vessel and its crew.

The *James A. McGean* disappeared in a swirl of foam that spewed out bits and pieces of wreckage and the bodies of the hapless men who had sailed in her.

Captain Chauncey Nye would not be home for his wedding anniversary. "Dancing Chauncey" Nye had danced his last waltz.

CHAPTER 11

"She Can't Be Pumped Out"

A FEW MILES BEHIND THE *MCGEAN*, the *Isaac M. Scott* rolled and pitched in the heavy seas. No one on the bridge saw the *McGean's* running lights disappear when she slipped beneath the waves; the spray and the blinding snow that lashed the pilothouse windows, sounding like buckshot striking a metal shed, prevented anyone from seeing much beyond the bowsprit of the 504-foot straight-deck freighter.

The *Scott* was but four years old, launched in Lorain, Ohio, June 12, 1909. She was owned by the Virginia Steamship Company and was under the management of the M. A. Hanna Company of Cleveland.

The boat was the twin of another lake steamer, the *Charles S. Price*, which on this Sunday was also upbound in Lake Huron, loaded with coal for Superior, Wisconsin. The *Scott* was bound for Milwaukee also with a load of coal.

The boat had always been under the command of Captain Archie McArthur, a peripatetic Scot who suffered a suspicion that other shipmasters held him responsible for the deaths of a dozen men four years earlier.

It had happened on the *Scott's* maiden voyage. In 1909 the new boat had collided in fogbound Whitefish Bay with the steamer *John B. Cowle*. The *Cowle* had sunk so quickly that most of her crew went down with her. With a huge hole in her bow, the *Scott* limped into the Soo. An investigation of the accident was conducted and Archie was called to explain his actions prior to the collision.

The investigating panel had determined that McArthur was blameless, but he couldn't seem to shake the feeling that all but a few of his colleagues were unconvinced.

But just now, he had other things to occupy his thoughts. The raging sea was mauling his boat mercilessly, and keeping her on course and out of the menacing troughs took all of his skill and that of his wheelsman, Edward E. Shipley. The vessel shrieked and moaned with every wave that twisted and stretched her hull; rivets were exploding out of her metal plates, sounding like an endless succession of rifle fire.

Each time a new wave struck her bow, the *Scott* shuddered; the heaving of the boat had McArthur and Shipley fighting to keep their footing, McArthur hanging on to the top rail on the ceiling of the pilothouse.

As the storm raged on, Captain Archie pondered over a choice he was being offered. The *Scott* was approaching the mouth of Thunder Bay on Michigan's eastern coast. He could turn into the bay and seek shelter until the storm blew out, or he could continue on up the lake, trusting in the boat's ability to take the punishment.

The season was nearing its end. The company bonus he would be paid was based heavily on the tonnage he was able to deliver during the year. And there was a degree of pride involved: Archie McArthur was not known for his timidness. He had never withered in the face of pressure. He was a "full steam ahead" master. Still, his unwillingness to pull back had contributed to the terrible collision in Whitefish Bay four years earlier. Steaming ahead in dense fog had resulted in the deaths of the men aboard the

Cowle. Whether he could be blamed or not for that regrettable loss of life, it might not have happened if he had dropped anchor—as other ships were doing that night— and waited until visibility was better.

The thought must have crossed his mind that visibility this night was no better, that the driving snow and windborne spray had left him as blind as he'd been the night of the collision. He had no way of knowing how many vessels might be in the bay, waiting for relief from this terrible weather. There was no radar in 1913, no radio direction finders to guide him safely into the bay. It was very possible that he could crash into an anchored steamer, put his boat on the rocks, tear her bottom out, and cast his crew into the frightful tempest. Out here on the lake, he was relatively safe: it was far less likely that he would run into another boat out in the middle of the lake.

Yes, he was better off where he was. The boat was riding reasonably well given the force of the cyclonic winds and pounding waves. The *Scott* was a young boat, strong and well constructed. Great care had been taken in her building, as evidenced by the beautifully polished brass in the wheelhouse and the rich, carved oak panels that adorned most spaces in her. Even the crew's quarters had the quality of a magnificent Tudor mansion.

Captain McArthur decided to put his faith in his boat—and his seamanship.

It is almost certain that the crew would have looked with beaming satisfaction at the thought of anchoring in the placid bay; there was no joy to be found in the writhing, pounding torment they and the boat were experiencing. Those in the forward part of the vessel would be looking forward to a long day and night without so much as a hot cup of coffee to cheer them if the boat continued on up the lake rather than anchoring in a quiet, calm harbor. Making one's way aft for something to eat was suicidal in this blow.

Not to say that crew members in the stern were enjoying themselves a great deal more. Rolling rods had been installed on the cook stoves to keep pots and pans from falling to the deck, and all cupboard doors and drawers were fastened shut. Unless there was a sudden break in the weather, only cold meats and vegetables would be served at the evening meal. The dining tables had been covered with wet cloths to help hold cups and dishes on the tabletops, and those who might choose to sit there were forced to eat with one hand and hold on tightly to something with the other.

Down in the engine room, stokers, coal passers, and oilers labored in miserable conditions. Under normal circumstances, the engine and boiler rooms were ventilated by air shafts that ran up along the inside of the smokestack. The stack was actually a double stack, with fresh air from topside supplied by way of the outer stack, while the smoke from the furnaces was pulled out of the engine and boiler rooms through the inner stack.

But the seventy-mile-an-hour winds blowing across the top of the stack now sucked the smoke out of the inner shaft and immediately drove it back down the outer shaft to the boiler room, where it filled the air, choking the crew below.

Just when it seemed that the black gang would be able to tolerate the conditions no longer, the problem of poor ventilation was solved. The engine room skylights were smashed in. Now the men were showered with icy water, soaking each to the skin, leaving them shivering in the cold.

Second Engineer Norman Dwelle, standing watch below, ordered a tarpaulin rigged just above the men to provide them with a degree of protection from the flood if not from the cold that now gripped the room.

Back on the bridge, Captain McArthur, standing at the pilothouse windows, straining to see beyond the bow, felt a sudden jolt accompanied by a crashing sound from the spar deck. Moving quickly to the chart room at the rear of the pilothouse, he peered out at the deck. The curtain of snow prevented him from seeing the after deck-house. But the deck lights offered just enough illumination to permit Archie to see what had caused the jolt and the crash. At least one of the hatch covers had either been carried away or smashed into the hold. In either event, the seas were now pouring into the vessel.

Dashing to the engine room speaking tube, he shouted down to Second Engineer Dwelle to start the pumps. It was, he knew, probably a futile gesture.

Within minutes word came back to him from below: "She can't be pumped out, captain."

Launching lifeboats in those seas was impossible: they would either be crushed against the side of the boat or be capsized the instant they hit the surface of the lake. And a man couldn't survive more than a few minutes in the frigid waters before hypothermia threw him into shock and unconsciousness and drowned him.

Archie McArthur's beautiful boat was going to sink, and twenty-eight men were doomed to go with her.

One of the twenty-eight was Albert Abram, of Chicago, a boatswain. Albert had intended this to be his last trip on the lakes; he had promised pretty Catherine Murphy that it would be.

Albert and Catherine were planning on a November 26 wedding.

The young woman had an abiding dislike for the lake boats that was grounded in an intense fear of deep water. And while she could love a sailor she absolutely would not marry one. When she had promised, several months earlier, to be Albert's wife, it was with the explicit understanding that he would leave the boats and seek some other occupation.

There was no pain or regret in promising to sail away no more; Albert had grown tired of the hardships and the danger found on the lakes.

And so it was with a sense of relief that he informed Captain McArthur, just before leaving Cleveland for Ashtabula to pick up a load of coal, that he would leave the *Scott* for good immediately on their return to Cleveland.

Albert Abram would keep his promise to Catherine to stop sailing the lakes, but he would not be leaving the *Scott*.

When the *Isaac M. Scott* came to rest on the bottom of Lake Huron in two hundred feet of murky water she had rolled over and landed on her top. The cargo of coal spilled out around her. A few of the dead crewmen floated to the surface, buoyed by life jackets hastily donned. But most remained with the boat, which now became their eternal tomb.

Archie McArthur would not be called on to explain his actions this time.

CHAPTER 12

"Boy, You're Going to See a Storm Such as You've Never Seen Before"

AT DETOUR ISLAND, THE *JAMES C. CARRUTHERS* filled her coal bunkers before heading down in Lake Huron.

Dockworkers recalled seeing First Mate William "Bill" Lediard supervising the loading. There was something different about the way he looked, something they couldn't quite put their finger on until sometime later. It was his moustache, or rather the absence of it. Lediard had shaved it off exactly a week earlier.

Some would later try to explain the disappearance by postulating that it was a subconscious attempt to get out of the shadow of William H. Wright, his skipper, who sported a most luxurious crop of flaming red facial hair. The forty-four-year-old first mate believed that he would soon be given his own command, and perhaps he did not want to look as though he were trying to copy Captain Wright.

Giving the tall, gaunt first mate his own boat made a great deal of sense. After all, he was a qualified and experienced master in his own right and the ship's owners had recently commissioned another vessel, an exact twin of the *Carruthers*.

It would not have been disingenuous to have recommended Captain Wright as an excellent role model. He had an intense interest in his job and took his responsibil-

78

ities to his boat, his crew, and his employers with extreme seriousness. The men who served under him not only respected the twenty-five-year-veteran mariner, they truly liked the man.

"He was everywhere on the boat," one crew member once commented. "When he wasn't on the bridge, he would be poking around in the windlass room or the galley or boiler room, always taking time to chat with the men, asking if everything was okay and listening carefully to any complaints."

When asked by a fellow shipmaster how he liked his new command, Wright commented: "We've still to learn all her tricks, and the lads in the fo'c'sle are complaining that the paint in their rooms is still sticky."

Wright and his wife had planned for her to make this trip with him on the *Carruthers*. It had become almost a tradition that she take the early November trip. But she had decided to postpone the voyage for a week to keep some commitments she'd made to their three children. It was agreed that she would meet the boat when it called at Port Colborne, Ontario, about November 15.

When she left DeTour Island, the *Carruthers* set a course for Georgian Bay, on the Canadian side, heading for the grain elevators at Midland.

Once in the lake, Captain Wright noted that the wind was freshening and snow was falling more heavily. He probably thought back to the heavy storm the *Carruthers* had come through on Superior two days before, and he may have recalled his comments to a member of his crew who was experiencing his first season on the Great Lakes. As the winds had begun to pick up in strength and the seas were mounting, Wright had seen a definite look of apprehension in the youngster's eyes.

"Get ready, son," he had told the crewman, "This is just the beginning. Boy, you're going to see a storm such as you've never seen before."

After reaching the Soo, the captain once again came upon the young man, still looking pale and drawn after his harrowing experience in the terrible storm.

"Well, lad, was I right about that blow?"

"You certainly were, captain. And I can only say, I hope I never see nothin' like it again."

"It's not likely, at least not this year."

"No, I suppose not."

Neither man realized it at the time but both would be wrong . . . fatally wrong.

The intensified gale struck the *Carruthers* in the early morning hours of November 9 with heavy, blinding snow. The winds were out of the north-northeast at fifty-five miles an hour. The *Carruthers*, heading for Georgian Bay, would have to make a critical turn to put it on a course into the bay. It was probably during this maneuver that she was caught broadside in a trough and the towering seas overwhelmed her. The barely five-month-old boat and her crew of twenty-four disappeared beneath the savage foam.

CHAPTER 13

"I'll Never Catch the Wexford"

JAMES MCCUTCHEON WAS IN A LATHER. He had missed his train by ten minutes, and it would be several hours before another one was scheduled. As he paced frantically about the Grand Trunk Railway station in Detroit, he muttered over and over: "I'll never catch the *Wexford*."

As first mate aboard the 250-foot packet freighter *Wexford*, he was attempting to join the boat at Sarnia, Ontario.

McCutcheon had left the boat when it had called at Windsor a few days earlier, downbound, planning to visit friends in Detroit. The *Wexford* was scheduled back in Windsor with a load of wheat, and McCutcheon's plan was to rejoin her there. However, at the last minute plans were changed and the freighter loaded steel rails instead, which were to be delivered at Fort William, Ontario.

But McCutcheon was late making the train and when he finally reached Port Huron—just across the St. Clair River from Sarnia—he discovered the boat had departed hours before.

Annoyed and disappointed, the mate would miss the trip, lose some pay, and mar a near-perfect record of dependability on the *Wexford*. Most of the crew of the small vessel had spent a good deal of time crewing her and took pride in their reliability.

The *Wexford* was a thirty-year-old packet freighter

that had been built by Doxford & Sons, Ltd. at Sunderland, England, in 1883 for service in the British Isles and Europe. Originally named *Wexford*, she was sold in 1898 to N. Dubuisson, a French shipping firm in Dunkirk, France, and renamed the *Elise*. In 1903, she was sold again, this time to the Western Steamship Company of Toronto, brought to the Great Lakes, and her original name—*Wexford*—restored.

Of different design than the traditional lake bulk carriers, slower and smaller, the boat carried whatever was available. Because it was of marginal importance in the Western Steamship Company's scheme of things, a marginally experienced skipper would serve their purposes. Therefore, twenty-six-year-old Captain Bruce Cameron was given the command.

The second son of the late Captain Alex C. Cameron of Collingwood, Ontario, Bruce came from a family of mariners. He had sailed the lakes since age sixteen and had successfully served in a number of capacities on several lake boats sailing out of Collingwood.

Newly married, Cameron was an exuberant young shipmaster who commanded a young and exuberant crew. Archibald Brooks, his second mate, was two years younger than the captain. McCutcheon, the absent first mate, was one year junior to Cameron. James Scott, the chief engineer, was one year older. Richard Lougheed, Allan Dodson, Orrin Gordon, and James Glenn (a pathetically homesick Scotsman who planned to return to Scotland to bring his wife back to Canada as soon as the season was over) were all in their early to mid-twenties. Only George Wilmont, the *Wexford*'s cook, was in his thirties.

While McCutcheon cooled his heels in Port Huron, his boat loaded grain up in Lake Superior for delivery to Goderich, Ontario.

While loading at Fort William, Cameron was approached by Murdoch and Donald McDonald, twenty-four-year-old cousins from Goderich.

Murdoch had been wheelsman on the *Turret Court* but took ill and decided to end the season and head for home. Donald had been on vacation, sailing north as a passenger aboard the same vessel.

But the boat was delayed at Fort William and Donald became worried that he wouldn't get home on time to return to his job. Returning to his job on schedule was most important to the young Donald McDonald; he was about to realize a dream of a lifetime. McDonald had worked for several years as a fireman on the Grand Trunk Railroad, and with every shovelful of coal he threw into the firebox of a locomotive his ambition grew to one day have his hand on the throttle of that locomotive as an engineer.

At long last, his dream had come true. Donald McDonald had been promoted to engineer. He had taken a week's vacation and was anxious to return to assume his new duties on a local run between Guelph and Hamilton, Ontario.

The pair requested passage aboard the *Wexford*, and the affable Cameron readily agreed.

The little steamer had been well constructed. She was designed to sail on any waters in any weather and had suffered the pounding of the storm on Lake Superior with no damage.

Once through the locks and down into Lake Huron, she hauled close into the Canadian shore, following the track of the *James C. Carruthers*. But rather than make the turn to close on Georgian Bay, the *Wexford* continued on down the lake.

Shortly before noon the steamer *Kaministiqua*, on her way up the lake, sighted the *Wexford* downbound approximately thirty miles north of the Goderich harbor.

At about two in the afternoon on November 9, a resident of the small Lake Huron town of Goderich who lived close to the harbor heard the sound of a ship's whistle blowing. He stated later that he did not hear the harbor foghorn at that time. The horn was supposed to have been sounding when the visibility dropped below certain minimums. On that Sunday afternoon, the fog was sufficiently thick that the horn should have been sounding.

Captain William Robinson, lighthouse keeper at Goderich, later insisted that the horn had been activated Friday afternoon and had sounded continuously throughout Sunday afternoon and night.

G. L. Parsons, superintendent of the Goderich Elevator and Transit Company, said it wouldn't have made any difference whether the horn was working or not. He said that he regarded the harbor as "inadequate as a harbor of refuge, that the fog horn was positioned in the wrong location to carry sound, was inadequately equipped and too weak for its purpose on such a wild night."

After a time the distress signals from the vessel ceased and the boat, which was not actually seen by the resident who heard the ship's whistle blowing or any other resident of the lake port town, apparently went away.

Many believe that the vessel blowing the distress signal was the *Wexford*, pleading for the horn to sound to assist it into the harbor and out of the terrible tumult that was then raging out on the lake.

No one knows for certain that the stricken vessel was indeed the little packet freighter *Wexford*. No one knows because the boat was never seen again. Days later the bodies of some of the crew members began to wash ashore not far from the town.

Ten days after the disappearance of the *Wexford*, a board washed ashore near Goderich. On the board was lettered a brief message which read "I am with the boat lashed to the wheel. —B"

It was assumed that "B" was Captain Bruce Cameron. His body was never found.

The McDonald cousins had, to be sure, gotten a ride back to Goderich, and James McCutcheon had missed the boat and a trip to eternity.

CHAPTER 14

"It Was a Rather Unpleasant Trip Down"

EARLY IN THE FIRST WEEK OF NOVEMBER 1913, with temperatures on Lake Huron in the high seventies and the surface almost like glass, more than one shipmaster had an ominous feeling that a terrible storm was going to strike sometime soon. The sky was a strange hue and an odd haze seemed to cover the sun, giving a surreal appearance to the lake.

Experienced mariners had seen this phenomenon before. It had always been the harbinger of bad things to come and made them want to get their vessels to a safe harbor as quickly as possible. What the omen promised need not strike immediately; it might be hours or even days away. But it was certainly coming.

There had been more violent winds on Lake Huron than those being experienced November 9th and 10th, but no one could remember them having continued for such an extended period. The seemingly ceaseless hurricane blasting the lake had caused gigantic seas to form that relentlessly pounded everything in their path. Waves struck boats in the lake, often sending spray to the top of the mast and tons of water crashing over decks and deckhouses. The persistent drop in temperature resulted in an accumulation of ice that clogged the scuppers and hawse pipes, leaving the lake water to accumulate on the decks.

There it froze, threatening the already overburdened boats.

Add to all of this the white curtain of snow that obscured everything and gave every indication of never stopping or even letting up. Most of the time, men on the bridge were unable to see the stern of their vessels because of the white cloud obscuring their vision.

It was no better on land. Along the Lake Huron coast, people were assaulted by winds coming off the lake that carried them off their feet and threatened to flatten buildings. Snow quickly piled in drifts. At Port Sanilac on the Michigan shore, the winds destroyed the city dock and tons of goods waiting to be shipped.

It was the same on the Canadian side of the lake. From the Bruce Peninsula south to Sarnia, the wind and snow made travel all but impossible and caused the loss of hundreds of farm livestock and the downing of telephone and telegraph lines. Beachfront homes were demolished in a number of places and damage to roofs and chimneys was widespread throughout the area.

Small craft, anchored in the harbors and inlets along the lake, were thrown against docks and up on the shore, splintered and crushed and battered.

Out on the lake, two ships—one upbound and one headed south—approached a spot, a relatively small part of Lake Huron, where the elements would overwhelm them.

The 416-foot *Argus*, under the command of Captain Paul Gutch, had passed Detroit at 5:40 P.M. Saturday, headed north with a load of coal.

Originally named the *Lewis Woodruff*, the *Argus* was built by the American Shipbuilding Company in Lorain, Ohio, for Gilchrest Transportation Company of Cleveland. Launched August 5, 1905, she sailed for Gilchrest until 1913, when she was sold to the Interlake Steamship Company. There her name was changed to *Argus* and she was turned over for management to Picands, Mather & Co., of Cleveland.

Meanwhile, locking down at the Soo at 9:30 Saturday night was the twin sister of the *Argus*, the *Hydrus*, loaded with ore and headed for Cleveland.

Also under the original ownership of the Gilchrest Transportation Company, she was launched at the American Shipbuilding yards on September 12, 1903. Christened as the *R. E. Schuck*, she was renamed *Hydrus* when bought by the Interlake Steamship Company along with the *Argus*.

Captain John H. Lowe, a native of Los Angeles, California, skippering the *Hydrus*, exhausted after his ordeal on Lake Superior, had described the trip to an acquaintance at the Soo by saying: "It was a rather unpleasant trip down." He couldn't know that the unpleasantness was just beginning.

Also serving on board were a pair of brothers, Kernol Christy, twenty-four, and his brother Leslie, twenty-one, both of Marine City, Michigan. The two had served on the boat throughout the 1913 season, Kernol as an oiler and Leslie as a fireman. Leslie's young wife had died in May, leaving a small baby.

After having followed the *Carruthers* and the *Sheadle* down from the Soo, the *Hydrus* found herself suddenly alone at the top of Lake Huron with a savage and violent hurricane building up to an uncontrolled fury.

Captain Lowe, nearing the point of total collapse, must have wondered what fates had conspired against him to call down such a disagreeable tempest to once again test the resolve he had shown hours earlier during the madness of Lake Superior.

Like so many sailors before him, he had ignored the storm signals that were prominently posted at the Soo, and like others he had ignored the barometer that told him bad weather was coming. It was said that some shipmasters actually hung their hats over the barometer so they wouldn't have to see what it was telling them.

Like so many masters, Lowe was sensitive to the fact that he commanded his boat at the pleasure of the owner—with the emphasis on *pleasure*. The storm of the past two days had cost him dearly in time. To heave to in the St. Marys River until there was no danger of additional heavy weather was a luxury no shipmaster dared enjoy. He would sail on, no matter the threat of the weather. He would make his scheduled delivery point on time . . . *or not at all!*

Ironically, not too many miles away, approaching from the south, also determined to reach port on schedule, was the *Argus*, suffering her own hellish punishment at the hands of the storm.

Somewhere between them, upbound in ballast, was the *George C. Crawford*, under the command of Captain Walter C. Iler.

The winds at this time were from the north, and Iler, without cargo, was having considerable difficulty maintaining steerageway. At one point he had managed to turn his boat around and head before the winds. But he feared he was being driven too close to land. During a brief lull, Iler swung the *Crawford* north once again.

Late Sunday afternoon the blinding snowstorm suddenly stopped for a few minutes. Iler, looking out at the lake and the rolling peaks and valleys of water, was seized with numbing horror. Ahead of him, perhaps two or three miles distant, was the *Argus*, caught in a deep trough and struggling like a wounded animal to get out.

As Iler watched, transfixed, the *Argus* "just appeared to crumble like an eggshell and then disappeared!"

Iler had his hands full trying to save his own vessel;

there was nothing he could do for the hapless souls in the *Argus*. The vision of the crumbling lake boat would haunt him as long as he lived.

Somewhere to the north, where no one was able to see, the *Hydrus*, probably just as suddenly, took her own fatal plunge to the lake bottom.

Each of the two boats carried a crew of twenty-three. They died on the same day—perhaps at the same instant—and they found their final resting place as close together as sister ships could expect to be.

CHAPTER 15

"They Took the Damned Coal"

THE HANNA TRANSIT COMPANY'S FIVE-HUNDRED-FOOT steamer *Howard M. Hanna Jr.* left Lorain, Ohio, on Saturday, November 8, 1913, loaded with 9,120 tons of soft coal to be delivered at Fort William, Ontario. She carried a crew of twenty-four men and a female cook.

The weather was nearly ideal—fair and clear with a moderate wind from the west—as she passed Port Huron and headed out into Lake Huron at 5:12 Sunday morning.

Captain William Hagan was in his cabin sleeping soundly, having left the standard message that he was to be awakened if there was any problem. The course Hagan had posted would take them near the center of the lake.

Hagan had either not seen or had not believed the weather bureau warnings of an impending heavy blow.

At 11:30 that morning, as the *Hanna* passed Harbor Beach, the wind, which had been holding steady from the west, began swinging erratically, first southeast and then a few minutes later northeast and finally north-northeast. The velocity began to increase rapidly, requiring Captain Hagan to order the wheelsman to haul more to north to keep the boat's head into the wind.

At about 3:00 P.M., as they struggled against the seas five miles off Pointe Aux Barques near Port Austin, Michigan, the snow increased from flurries to a heavy fall.

Hagan notified his chief engineer to give him full steam. The vessel was barely making headway and the mounting waves crashing into her were causing water to flood into the boat. The siphons and pumps had to be started to control the intake. Canvas was strung over the electric dynamo to insure that the pumps were not put out of commission.

Things seemed to stabilize until three and a half hours after the weather turned worse.

"About 6:30 P.M., the bloody destruction began," Chief Engineer Frank Mayberry remembered later. "The oiler's door on the starboard side was the first to get smashed in, and shortly afterward the two engine room doors and windows went. It was terrible. Tons of icy water were pouring into the engine room. The whole place was a damned mess. We stood knee-deep in the swirling water and more kept rushing in."

Captain Hagan called down to ask if the engine was working all right and Mayberry assured him it was.

"We mustn't yield to the weather," Hagan said. "We need all the power we can possibly get to keep this craft headed into the wind."

At 7:30 P.M. the windows and doors of the engineer's room crashed in.

"That must have opened the breach," Mayberry said. "After that it seemed as if everything else went in order."

The cook's room and the dining room went, and the woodwork was torn away and dropped into the engine room to add to the wreckage already piling up there. Amid the flotsam roaring down from the cook's room was the cook herself. The startled engine-room crew watched as diminutive, 103-pound Sadie Black—the wife of steward Clarence Black—was unceremoniously deposited one deck down in the engine room along with the furnishings of her room.

Conditions above deck were growing steadily worse.

"Tremendous seas were coming over our bow and starboard quarters, over the whole vessel in fact," Captain Hagan reported later.

The waves carried away part of the after cabin, smashed in the windows and doors of the pilothouse, and ripped away its roof. The *Hanna* began falling off her course and the men on the bridge were helpless to stop it.

"Between 7:00 and 8:00 P.M., it was snowing so hard we couldn't see land," Hagan said. "It was impossible to judge our exact position or gauge our speed, but we must have been about fifteen miles off Pointe Aux Barques."

Shortly after, the boat fell off into a trough and began to roll heavily with the waves washing over her.

"Can't we do anything?" the crew wanted to know.

"I don't know of anything more we could have done," Mayberry said. "The engine room crew did their best, even when water was coming in in torrents."

As the confusion and chaos mounted a new threat was approaching.

Shortly before 10:00 P.M., the men on the bridge saw the Port Austin light and realized they had drifted dangerously close to the reef.

Captain Hagan ordered the first mate to go to the forward windlass room and drop the *Hanna*'s anchors. Both forward hooks were dropped but failed to catch and the boat continued drifting toward the rocks.

At 10:00 P.M., with a terrible grinding, crunching sound and a frightening lurch, the *Howard M. Hanna Jr.* was thrust broadside into the reef, her port side stove in. The next few waves drove her all the way up on the rocks. She listed badly to starboard, the waves roaring in to tear her hatches away. The smokestack tilted precariously and was blown into the snow-filled night.

Through the hours, those trapped in the forward section and those unable to get out of the after cabins waited in terror with no means of communication between the two ends of the vessel.

The messroom and kitchen were still intact—although at times water was waist-deep in both places—and Sadie Black struggled to keep a fire in the stove and served hot coffee to the men there throughout Sunday night and into Monday. In the afternoon of Monday, when the weather moderated slightly, the third engineer managed to make his way forward, bringing much-appreciated food for those stranded in the Texas deck cabins just below the bridge.

Tuesday morning the forward crewmen scrambled aft to join the others in the kitchen. As they moved across the spar deck on their way aft, the men noticed that the boat had a crack across the deck and down the side—she was in danger of breaking in two. In addition to the missing smokestack, the life rafts and the starboard lifeboat had disappeared.

With the ship obviously breaking up around them, the crew nervously pondered over the possibility of rescue. Distress rockets had been fired, but in the blinding snowstorm and the spray, they could not be certain their call for help had been seen.

As a matter of fact, the signals were spotted about 8:30 Monday morning by the Port Austin lifesaving crew during a lull in the blizzard. But getting out to the stricken vessel was no easy matter. Their boathouse and dock had been destroyed and their surfboat buried in the sand. They managed to launch a small lifeboat, but a half mile out the lifeboat filled with water, forcing them to beat a hasty retreat for shore.

Surfman Number One Thomas Deegan was dispatched to Port Austin to telephone the lifesaving stations at Harbor Beach and Huron City to ask that help be sent immediately.

But those stations were having their own wrecks to

deal with. There were four wrecks waiting for assistance from the Harbor Beach station alone.

With no help forthcoming from other quarters, the Port Austin crew set about exhuming their buried surf-boat. But when they had managed to dig the small boat out of the sand, they discovered that the gunwale was broken in five places and the boat had numerous holes in her bottom. It was late Monday night before they had succeeded patching all the tears.

Unaware of the lifesaving crew's efforts on their behalf, some of the men aboard the *Hanna* decided to take matters into their own hands.

At daylight Tuesday, several of the men had gone on deck and cleared the water and the accumulated ice from the port side lifeboat—the only one that had not been ripped away by the storm—and, at 7:30 A.M., succeeded in launching it.

Nine members of the crew started for shore to seek help. It was two and a half hours later when the lifeboat from shore met the men in the *Hanna*'s lifeboat trying desperately to make the beach in the thundering seas.

The lifesavers took six men and Sadie Black off the broken and battered *Hanna*. Sadie put up a struggle before abandoning the boat.

"When it came time for us to leave and get into the lifesaver's boat Mrs. Black refused the courtesies extended to a woman in time of danger at sea," Boatswain Arthur Jacobs recalled later. "She took her turn in the order of her position and went over the side clad in the fireman's heavy shoes."

She had lost all her clothes, her jewelry, and $150 in cash. Later, the members of the boat's crew, in appreciation for her dedication and courage during the grueling ordeal, took up a personal collection and, in the words of Boatswain Jacobs, "Filled a purse for Sadie."

She was so seriously affected by the exposure to the icy waters and the terrible cold that the lifesavers were genuinely concerned that she might not reach shore alive.

The patched-up surfboat leaked so terribly that the lifesaving crew paddled frantically to make shore before sinking.

Residents of Port Austin were waiting on shore, ready to receive the exhausted, demoralized, and physically spent *Hanna* crew members.

The near-frozen survivors were rushed to the homes of worried townspeople to dry them out and warm them up. Hot coffee by the gallon was passed around and then they were taken to a local hotel for a hot, substantial meal.

Meanwhile the lifesavers returned one final time to the broken freighter to rescue the remaining members of the crew. Again frantically bailing the surfboat, the lifesavers took the crewmen still on board. This time they hoisted a sail to help speed them to shore.

The balance of the *Hanna*'s crew were taken and warmed, as the others had been, and then rushed off to join their comrades in the first hot meal they'd enjoyed in almost forty-eight hours.

Eventually they were returned to Cleveland, their home port, where they regaled family and friends with animated accounts of the frightful, death-defying experiences they had lived through in the worst storm on the Great Lakes anyone had ever known.

Most stayed with the company and returned to the lakes the following season on other boats, always to feel a sense of apprehension when the gales of November threatened. A few, such as Clarence and Sadie Black, left the lakes forever.

The fifteen-year-old *Howard M. Hanna Jr.*, now dark and crewless, lay broken and alone on the barren reef where she would stay throughout the long, cold windswept winter. The following spring marine inspectors toured the wreck and declared the remnants of the young lake steamer valued at $301,155, a total loss.

She was sold for scrap. But miraculously the salvager refloated the hulk and towed her to Collingwood, where she was repaired and refitted. She continued to sail the lakes for many years under a number of different names before finally making the scrap pile in the mid-1980s.

While the *Hanna* may have been abandoned by her crew, her captain, and to a large extent her company, she was not forgotten by some of the more enterprising members of the Port Austin community. After all, she was loaded with over nine thousand tons of coal.

Incredibly, throughout the winter the full eighteen million-plus pounds of soft coal was systematically off-loaded from the hulk balanced precariously on a reef a mile and a half out in the lake.

"They took the damned coal?" an astounded insurance adjuster thundered in disbelief.

Clarence Black, the former *Hanna* steward, visited the site of his most frightening experience some ten years after the last terrible days he had served aboard the boat. Having left the lake boats—as he had planned to well before the wreck—and gone into private business with his wife, Sadie, in Cleveland, he was drawn to the place that held such dramatic memories for him.

He came away with a remarkable discovery regarding the purloined coal.

"Ten years after the wreck, imagine that, ten years after the wreck, there were people in that town who were *still* burning that coal."

CHAPTER 16

"The Whereabouts of the Regina Will Forever Be a Mystery"

HE LOVED COMMAND. HE LOVED THE FEELING he got as he stood on the wing of the tiny bridge and called out directions to his most trusted wheelsman, twenty-two-year-old Bob Stalker, watching protectively as the steamer slowly edged to a berth in one of the harbors on Canada's north shore.

Captain Ed McConkey was master of the *Regina*, a package freighter owned by the Canadian Interlake Line of Montreal, Quebec. She had been built in Dumbarton, Scotland, in 1907 for C. H. F. Plummer, a Montreal shipping firm, and brought to the Great Lakes to make the run between Montreal and Fort William.

In 1911 she was sold to the Canadian Lake Transportation Company and again in 1912 to Canadian Interlake.

A resident of Barrie, Ontario, young, ambitious McConkey was completing his first shipping season as a shipmaster. It was also his first season aboard the *Regina*.

The boat was not an imposing vessel. She had few of the fancy appointments, lush carved oak paneling, and luxurious quarters found on the larger lake boats. Her pilothouse was small and cramped, with hardly enough room for the master and a wheelsman to stand and still have space for a small chart table. But she was home to the feisty little Irishman and to her fifteen-man crew.

She measured just 249 feet and 3 inches in length, and she had a gross tonnage of 1,956 tons. Her shallow draft made it possible for her to get into many lake ports that were unserviceable to most of the larger lake freighters, and McConkey liked that just fine. He enjoyed calling at the numerous small and difficult harbors, deriving great satisfaction in maneuvering his craft in the tight spots. He never tired of it.

Much of the cargo the small freighter carried included general merchandise, whiskey, wine, cheese, fencing, barbed wire, and a multitude of other small items residents of the villages and towns of Ontario needed or wanted to buy.

Shortly before seven o'clock Sunday morning, November 9, 1913, the *Regina* cast off her lines from the dock at Sarnia, drifted into the current of the St. Clair River, and slowly steamed north into Lake Huron. McConkey's orders called for stops at seven ports on the Canadian side of Lake Huron and Lake Superior. The trip was to take approximately ten days.

Partially loaded when she arrived at Sarnia, the *Regina* took on an additional eight railroad cars of canned goods from Leamington, Ontario, and a selection of manufactured goods from Sarnia, Chatham, and Dresden companies. The manufactured goods included a load of steel sewer and gas pipes that protruded above the boat's rails, which prompted Danny Lynn of the Lynn Marine Reporting Company to later comment that the deck cargo the *Regina* carried "looked dangerous. She appeared topheavy."

Included in the deck load—which had been supervised by First Mate Wesley Adams—was 140 tons of baled hay, covered with tarpaulins secured to the deck plating.

On his second trip aboard the package steamer was oiler Dave Lawson, who had originally signed on for just one voyage, planning to sail to Fort William and then work his way west to Winnipeg. But for some reason he never explained to his shipmates, he decided to stay on for an indefinite period.

While the *Regina* may not have boasted the comparatively plush surroundings of the bigger boats, the crew members tended to covet their berths aboard her. Because it was a small boat with a smaller than usual complement of men, there was a relaxed informality about the boat, and Captain McConkey was not one to hold himself aloof from the rest of the crew. He expected a full measure of work from his men, and as long as everyone pulled his weight things went smoothly.

One member of the crew was not aboard as the *Regina* steamed into Lake Huron that November Sunday morning. Three weeks earlier, George Gosby, a watchman from Toronto, had tripped on a hatch cover and had fallen into a cargo hold, breaking a leg.

"Just my luck," he had complained as he was gingerly lifted out. "I break a leg and miss the rest of the season."

As had been observed by Captain Hagan of the *Howard M. Hanna*, the wind shifted at 11:30 A.M. from the west to the north-northeast and increased in strength until about two the next morning, when it moved around to the northeast. The wind velocity had held at an average speed of sixty miles an hour for twelve hours, although Captain Lyons of the *J. H. Sheadle* reported that he had experienced seventy-mile-an-hour winds off Harbor Beach. Wave heights during this period were said to have exceeded thirty-five feet.

In spite of the terrible seas and the battering winds, the *Regina* continued plowing along on her northern course.

She was sighted at about 1:30 P.M. by Captain Arthur May of the *H. B. Hawgood*, who recalled seeing her about fifteen miles south of Harbor Beach with "seas breaking over her."

At least one theorist believes that at about this time
Captain McConkey, conscious of the dangers posed by the
top-heavy cargo load he carried on his decks, decided that
continuing on in a storm that seemed to have no end and
in seas that threatened to mount ever higher was madness.

Ordering the *Regina* to put about, McConkey hoped
to be able to make it back to the St. Clair River and safe
refuge.

But, as she tried to make the turn, the *Regina*, according to the theory, was caught in a wave trough much
as the *Hanna* had been. Caught in the trough, the boat
was carried down the lake. McConkey ordered the starboard anchor dropped, hoping to be able to pull her bow
around and into the wave path. But the anchor dragged
along the bottom, failing to catch and hold.

Attempts to straighten the boat by running her engine at full speed proved equally unsuccessful because the
wave movement from the northwest combined with winds
blowing out of the northeast to exert a weather-vane effect
on the vessel that kept her broadside in the troughs.

From the spot of the sighting by the steamer *Hawgood* south of Harbor Beach, the *Regina* was driven over
fifteen miles south to a point just off Port Sanilac.

The constant pounding of the waves on the *Regina*'s
spar deck would eventually have caused the cargo stored
there to break loose and for hatch covers to be torn away.
The hull also would have begun to buckle under the terrible punishment the boat was taking.

With the pumps unable to manage the tremendous
flood that was coming inside, Captain McConkey would
have recognized the inevitable and given the order to
abandon ship.

The pilothouse and engine-room chadburns were
moved to the *ALL STOP* position and the engines shut
down to avoid additional dangers from the propeller while
quitting the boat.

Attempts were made to launch the pair of lifeboats carried topside, but only one managed to stay afloat. When it washed ashore several days later it contained the bodies of oiler David M. Lawson—who originally had planned to make but one trip aboard the boat but had decided to stay on—fireman Gustave Oleson, and Chief Engineer C. J. McSorley.

As her hull filled with water, she began to list to starboard. More water poured onto her deck as the waves continued to pound her sides. Her topside cargo was washed overboard, and as it slid over the rail it contributed more to the tilt of the vessel until she lay fully on her starboard side in the valley of a wave, finally settling below the surface and continuing to twist over.

There is evidence to indicate that the *Regina* went down at 4:20 A.M., November 10, 1913, in eighty feet of water, coming to rest almost fully bottom-side up, resting partially on her starboard side. Her hull broke at a point about ninety-five feet from the rudder post. Her starboard anchor chain stretched out from the wreck, pointing in a north-northeasterly direction.

Some cargo remained inside the hull. Crates containing bottles and canned goods were strewn along the lake floor near the wreck. The wooden pilothouse was totally destroyed. Only a single length of pipe was nearby, the balance of the sewer and gas pipes having been lost prior to her foundering.

Great quantities of cans and bottles and other bits and pieces of cargo floated to the surface and began the long journey east across the lake to the Canadian shore.

By the time the storm had died and travel over the lakes was once again safe, no sign of the *Regina*'s grave site could be found. A representative of the ship's owners, when asked where he thought the boat might have sunk, replied: "The whereabouts of the *Regina* will forever be a mystery."

CHAPTER 17

"Oh, Come with Me, Arz, Come with Me"

IN MILWAUKEE, WISCONSIN, pretty Minnie Dobbins read for the third—or possibly the fourth—time the latest letter from her fiancé, Ives Morey, a tall, handsome Detroiter.

Minnie and Ives had met during one of his visits to Milwaukee. He'd been introduced to her by the sister of one of his close friends. Both tended to be somewhat shy, introspective people who had not found making friends easy or natural, as so many of their acquaintances seemed to do.

They were both avid readers of books. Minnie, a secretary for the assistant vice president of a Milwaukee bank, tended to be attracted to philosophical literature—the thirteenth-century philosopher and theologian Saint Thomas Aquinas, Benedict de Spinoza, and George Santayana were among her favorites. Ives was partial to books dealing with American history and outdoor adventure thrillers—particularly the works of Jack London.

It had been love at first sight and the couple planned a wedding in early 1914. She visited Detroit several times to meet and spend time with his widowed mother. And he was a regular visitor at the Dobbins household.

Hardly a week went by that Minnie didn't receive at least one letter from Ives. It wasn't as easy for her to write to him: he was a Great Lakes sailor who spent nine months a year at sea. Minnie would write to him at his mother's address and then have to wait for him to call at Detroit to receive the letters.

Unlike Catherine Murphy—also from Milwaukee—who refused to marry Albert Abram if he continued working the lake boats, Minnie Dobbins wasn't especially bothered by Ives's choice of career, even though it meant he would be gone much of the time. In fact, she found it somewhat glamorous and looked forward to the time when they were wed and she would have the opportunity, as many relatives of crew members did, to take one or two trips on board his boat.

As the season moved into its final month, Minnie did become a bit apprehensive. Ives had told her about the storms that struck when November visited the lakes. But he didn't seem to worry about it; his was a sturdy boat, barely three years old. Over five hundred feet in length and considered among the very best and the safest freighters to sail the lakes, she was named the *Charles S. Price*.

At least one other woman wasn't worried about her husband being a Great Lakes sailor. Thirty-two-year-old Margaret Jones was so comfortable with his job that she accompanied him on the latest trip down from Superior, Wisconsin, where they made their home. She and Herbert, thirty-four, the *Price*'s steward, had recently been married and this was to be their honeymoon cruise.

Owned by the Mahoning Steamship Company, the *Price* was managed by the M. A. Hanna Company of Cleveland and under the command of Captain William A. Black, a veteran shipmaster who had skippered the *Price* for just one season. Prior to the *Price*, Black had spent two seasons as master of the Hanna boat *W. A. Fitch*. Prior to that he had commanded the company's barge *Maitland*. He was a member of the Shipmasters' Association and resided during the off-season in Cleveland.

The *Price* was the pride of the company, the jewel of the lakes. Those who crewed her tended to stay with her season after season. When, after an illness or an injury, crew members were "left on the beach" for one trip or more, they tended to worry whether or not they would be able to retrieve their berth aboard her. It was virtually unheard of for a member of the *Price*'s crew to voluntarily quit the boat before the season was over.

This was clearly in Assistant Engineer Milton Smith's mind as he sat whiling away the time while the *Price* was loading coal in Ashtabula, Ohio.

Something had nagged at him the last few days; he couldn't put a finger on it, it seemed to be a voice in his head telling him that he should leave the boat immediately.

"I was getting tired of sailing anyway," Smith would insist later. "I wanted to get away from it."

His wife had urged him to return home to Port Huron, Michigan, to be with the family.

He was looking for some justifiable excuse to quit the boat but could come up with nothing more concrete than this insistent premonition that something terrible would happen to him if he remained aboard.

He checked a Cleveland newspaper, perhaps hoping that there would be something there to buttress his feeling that he should go ashore. Nothing caught his eye.

Finally, he threw up his hands and thought, "I've got to get off this boat and this is the best chance I will have."

He went to his superior officer, Chief Engineer John Groundwater, who also happened to be a close personal friend.

"John, I decided I'm going to end the season now. I'm going home."

"What?" the stunned Groundwater said. "Get that wild hair out of your nose and stick around. Why throw

The Charles S. Price in the St. Clair River in 1912. Inset: Called the "mystery ship," the Charles S. Price was found floating upside down north of Port Huron, Michigan. It was nearly a week after the great storm before it was positively identified. (Photos courtesy of the Institute for Great Lakes Research, Bowling Green State University)

Originally christened the R. E. Schuck, it was later renamed the Hydrus. Inset: The Argus, sister ship of the Hydrus. The two ships went down in Lake Huron during the same storm, on the same day and very close to each other. (Photos courtesy of the Institute for Great Lakes Research, Bowling Green State University)

The Henry B. Smith at her launching in Lorain, Ohio, May 2, 1906. (Photo courtesy of the Institute for Great Lakes Research, Bowling Green State University)

The Isaac M. Scott *sometime in 1910. (Photo courtesy of the Institute for Great Lakes Research, Bowling Green State University)*

The Leafield, the first vessel to sink in the storm of November 1913. (Photo courtesy of the Institute for Great Lakes Research, Bowling Green State University)

The James C. Carruthers, lost with all hands on Lake Huron. (Photo courtesy of the Institute for Great Lakes Research, Bowling Green State University)

The Regina. The body of a crewman from the Charles S. Price was found wearing a life jacket from the Regina, creating a mystery that has never been solved. (Photo courtesy of the Institute for Great Lakes Research, Bowling Green State University)

The John A. McGean. Her skipper was nicknamed "Dancing Chauncey" Nye. (Photo courtesy of the Institute for Great Lakes Research, Bowling Green State University)

Lightship Number 82, sunk in Lake Erie near Buffalo.
Inset: The hulk of Lightship Number 82 was raised from the
bottom of Lake Erie in 1914. She was rebuilt and returned to
service. (Photos courtesy of the Institute for Great Lakes Research, Bowling
Green State University)

The Huronic. A Great Lakes cruise ship that was caught in the storm on Lake Superior but made it to shelter. (Photo courtesy of the Institute for Great Lakes Research, Bowling Green State University)

Built in England, the Wexford was brought to the Great Lakes as a "package freighter" to call on the smaller Great Lakes ports. Inset: Oars and other debris from the Regina and the Wexford washed up on the Canadian shore after the storm of 1913.
(Photos courtesy of the Institute for Great Lakes Research, Bowling Green State University)

Life preservers collected after the storm of November 1913 had piled up behind the Brophey & Son undertakers building in Goderich, Ontario. (Photo courtesy of the Institute for Great Lakes Research, Bowling Green State University)

Bodies from the Wexford washed ashore near Goderich, Ontario. (Photo courtesy of the Institute for Great Lakes Research, Bowling Green State University)

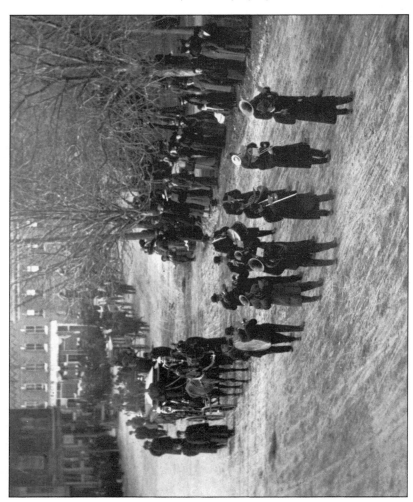

A funeral procession moves through the town square at Goderich, Ontario. The horse-drawn hearses bear the bodies of five unidentified sailors. *(Photo courtesy of the Institute for Great Lakes Research, Bowling Green State University)*

The graves of the five unidentified sailors in Maitland Cemetery near Goderich, Ontario. The bodies were later consolidated in one large grave and a single marker placed over it. (Photo courtesy of the Institute for Great Lakes Research, Bowling Green State University)

The permanent monument in Maitland Cemetery near Goderich, Ontario, to the memories of the unidentified seamen who died in the storm of November 1913. (Author photo)

money in the bilge? The *Price* will be tied up for the winter inside of three weeks and you'll collect your crew bonus on top of your regular pay. Take my advice son. Think it over."

By this time Smith was determined. He would get off the boat while the getting was good. He packed his belongings and asked for his time.

His shipmates, hearing of his sudden departure because of a premonition, ridiculed him for leaving with the end of the season so near. Others laughed, some scoffed at him, and some made insulting remarks about his mental state.

Arz McIntosh, a wheelsman, heard of Smith's decision and approached him.

"Milt, is it true that you're going to leave the boat?"

Smith allowed that it was true.

"Damn it! I wish I was going with you."

Arz had been having eye problems and desperately wanted to go home to have the difficulties corrected.

"Oh, come with me, Arz. Come with me," Smith pleaded.

But in the end, McIntosh decided that he would stick it out for one or two more trips.

When Smith disembarked from the *Price* he left the Cleveland newspaper he had been scanning while trying to firm his decision.

On an open page was the weather report for the next two days. It read, "November 8, 1913—Snow or rain and colder Saturday, with west to southwest winds. *Sunday, unsettled.*"

Bert L. Reynolds of Cleveland was quickly recruited to fill Smith's spot before the *Price* sailed.

Evelyn Mackley stood at the window of the small cottage she shared with her husband, Howard, watching downriver for the lights of a steamer making its way up the St. Clair River. It was shortly after 6:00 A.M. and she had been patiently waiting in this spot for almost an hour.

Suddenly, the low moan of a ship's whistle drifted up from the river. She sprang through the door and dashed across the lawn to the river's edge, peering through a light rain and freshening winds into the darkness.

Then she saw it, the hulking form of a huge freighter moving slowly into view. Evelyn watched as the boat drew abreast of where she waited. On top of the boat's pilot-house Evelyn saw what she had been waiting for. Howard was standing there, waving to her. He pulled on a lanyard and the boat's whistle tooted a greeting to her. She waved excitedly as the freighter plowed up the river before it disappeared once again in the predawn darkness and was gone.

The freighter was the *Charles S. Price* and Howard was her second mate. The scene just played out on a stretch of the St. Clair River just below Port Huron was re-created each time the *Price* passed. Howard always let Evelyn know about what time the boat would be coming by, and she never failed to be out waiting to catch a glimpse of him and to wave.

The young couple had been married seventeen months. But to friends and family who watched them with undisguised glee, they were still like newlyweds on their honeymoon.

Howard had sailed the *Price* all season with the exception of a short time when he filled in for another second mate on the *Leonard Hanna*. He loved his berth aboard the new steamer and had proudly taken Evelyn with him on several trips during the season. The affable young woman enjoyed these cruises very much and quickly made friends with several members of the crew including John Groundwater and steward Jones.

The *Price* moved into Lake Huron just a few miles behind the *Howard M. Hanna Jr*, the *Isaac M. Scott*, and the *Regina*. She was assaulted by the same strong winds and growing seas that struck the others.

In the early hours of Monday, November 10, the steamer *H. B. Hawgood*, plowing south, trying to make the safety of the St. Clair River, met the *Price* just north of Harbor Beach, still headed into the storm and "making bad weather of it."

It has been speculated that sometime shortly after this meeting, Captain Black decided to haul about and make a run for safety. Successfully negotiating the turn, the *Price* followed the *Hawgood* south and, so the theory goes, was somehow caught in yet another trough. With the boat rolling precipitously, the load of coal began to shift, causing her to heel far over to the side to be caught there by a large wave. The unstable vessel was thrust over, and her nine-thousand-ton cargo crashed out of the hold and spilled to the floor of the lake below. A mountain of coal would later be found some two miles from where the boat would finally come to rest.

The *Charles S. Price* capsized so quickly that the crew was caught totally unprepared, given no time to attempt to launch lifeboats or even to don heavy clothing to help protect them from the frigid waters into which they were cast.

PART IV
THE END OF IT

CHAPTER 18

"Good-By, Nellie"

ON SUNDAY MORNING AND AFTERNOON, the eastern shore of Lake Erie was experiencing moderate winds from the north and east. But by 3:30 A.M. Monday morning the winds had grown in strength from the south, and they raged on for fifteen hours accompanied by an unusually heavy snowfall.

In Buffalo, U.S. Weather Bureau forecaster David Cuthbertson saw something ominous in the sudden and unexpected meteorological anomaly. He quickly telephoned shipping companies and loading docks to advise them that movement by any vessel on Lake Erie for the next several hours could be extremely hazardous.

A violent storm was already beginning to batter all of northern Ohio, Pennsylvania, and New York with strong winds, heavy snow, and blizzard-like conditions. Telephone and telegraph lines were falling all along the Lake Erie shoreline. It didn't take a genius to realize that forecaster Cuthbertson's warning was not the ranting of a hysterical bureaucrat. More than thirty commercial vessels remained safely at anchor behind the breakwaters waiting for clearance to depart.

One vessel already on Lake Erie could not be reached—and it wouldn't have mattered a great deal if it could, because it would not have returned to port under any circumstances.

111

The United States *Lightship Number 82* was stationed in Lake Erie near Point Albino, thirteen miles west of Buffalo, standing guard over the shallows on the Canadian side as well as keeping watch on the lighted buoy positioned over the wreck of the *W. C. Richardson*, which had gone down a number of years earlier and now lay rusting and rotting on the bottom just below the surface of the lake, posing a danger to navigation should the lighted buoy somehow break loose or its light go out.

The lightship was under the command of Captain Hugh Williams, a native of Manistee, Michigan. Tranquil in nature, Williams was nevertheless dedicated to his command.

To be sure, his command would win no marine beauty prize: it had the appearance of a grotesque sausage with a gigantic toothpick driven in the top on which had been fastened a light. Officially designated as United States *Lighthouse Ship Number 82 (USLHS 82)*, she had been built the year before by the Racine-Truscott-Shell Boat Company at Muskegon, Michigan. She was of all-steel construction with an overall length of eighty feet and a displacement of 187 tons. She was owned by the United States Lighthouse Service.

Designed to withstand the worst possible weather, her official mission was to be anchored over a designated spot and to remain there no matter what the weather or sea conditions. To maintain a specific position, *Lightship 82* was equipped with four-ton mushroom anchors, fore and aft secured by heavy wrought-iron steel chains made to the most exacting specifications. To control the strain on these chains, *Lightship 82* was powered by a coal-fired engine. A strong steel mast was topped by a brilliant beacon to warn away vessels seeking safety in a storm.

The vessel was of adequate size to house a six-man crew—with a galley and sleeping quarters—for extended periods of time.

On the night of November 10, in addition to Captain Williams, the lightship's crew consisted of Mate Andrew Leahy and Assistant Engineer Cornelius Leahy, both of Elyria, Ohio; Engineer Charles Butler and cook Peter Mackey, both from Buffalo; and William Jensen, of Muskegon, Michigan.

At about 3:20 A.M. November 11, Captain Fred A. Dupuie was on the bridge of the steamer *Champlain*, which was loaded with grain and inbound for Buffalo. The boat had battled its way across Lake Erie through sixty- and seventy-mile-an-hour winds and a murderous following sea that, typical of the shallow lake, had come in rapid succession, subjecting the vessel to a terrible pounding.

As the *Champlain* neared the harbor entrance at Buffalo, Captain Dupuie became quite concerned. He was not able to pick out the light at Point Albino that would warn him of the shoal area and also confirm the fact that he was exactly thirteen miles from the harbor. Dupuie finally came to the conclusion that the lightship had hove anchor and run for shelter. He decided that it would have been a prudent move under the weather conditions then on the lake.

But later, when Dupuie reported to the harbormaster in Buffalo, he expressed concern for the absent lightship.

"The lightship was gone when we passed her anchorage this morning," he said. "There was no sign of her and we decided that the boat had either gone to the bottom or had run for shelter. The fact that the lightship is not in port strengthens our fear early this morning that she was driven from her anchorage and went to the bottom."

Such a suggestion seemed preposterous to the harbormaster. It was unthinkable that the sturdy lightship could have been overwhelmed by any storm, no matter its magnitude. Only once before had a lightship been blown off its moorings, and that vessel had not been equipped with the kind of mushroom anchors installed on *Lightship 82*.

But later in the day bits and pieces of wreckage began washing up in Buffalo: a piece of railing with *USLHS 82* painted on it, some cabin paneling, and at least one drawer that was identified as having come from the light-ship.

A few days later Frank Fleisner, walking along the shore near Buffalo, found a life preserver stenciled with the inscription *"Lightvessel No. 82."* Also found in the same general area was a piece of board, possibly from a door, on which had been scrawled a most poignant confirmation of the tragic fate of the lightship. It read "Good-by, Nellie, the ship is breaking up fast. Williams."

None of the six-man crew survived the fierce storm on Lake Erie. The lifeless body of Captain Hugh Williams washed ashore a few days later.

In the spring of 1914, the hulk of *Lightship 82* was discovered and raised by the Reid Wrecking Company. By 1915, she had been rebuilt and restored to service. In 1937 she was dropped from the U.S. Lighthouse Service list of vessels.

CHAPTER 19

"A Terrible Price Has Been Paid"

THE SAVAGELY DESTRUCTIVE STORM that had plundered much of the Great Lakes area had left the residents largely out of touch with what was happening elsewhere. In many cases information was sparse about what had occurred in their own communities.

The focus of interest among those just digging out from under the heavy snow and ice was the damage that occurred to property. The survivors of the blizzard concentrated on what had happened to them and their communities.

Those living in lake port cities and towns who had some connection, no matter how flimsy, with the shipping industry and lake commerce were, to be sure, concerned about those who had been caught out in the storm.

But most were confident that shipmasters would have taken shelter and waited for the winds to abate before venturing back on the open water. In any event, they were content to wait for whatever news was forthcoming. And the news was slow in arriving.

There was no television or even radio in 1913. Information supply, on a mass scale, was the sole property of newspapers. And reports coming over the telegraph and telephone wires were at first meager, conflicting, often unverified, and frequently blatantly untrue, causing a great deal of unnecessary anxiety and fear among families and friends of men out on the lakes.

To be sure, there were accurate newspaper accounts of the havoc on the lakes. But these dealt with vessels that had gone aground, were located, and whose crews had been rescued. The first newspaper story to mention what had happened and was continuing to happen on the lakes themselves appeared on November 10 and dealt with the wreck of the steamer *Louisiana* in Lake Michigan. Another report that same day mentioned that the steamer *Leafield* was missing in Lake Superior and was believed to have been lost with all hands.

The following day the newspaper headlines began announcing reports of a number of boats that had failed to make port and could not be located. There were also accounts of many large steamers having been driven aground in Lake Huron and that at least one was lost, perhaps with all her crew.

The lost lake steamer was unnamed. It was discovered by several other boats fighting their way south out of storm-tossed Lake Huron. Shipmasters were reporting sighting part of the overturned hull of a large steamer floating several miles north of Port Huron near the Gratiot light.

The boat drew national attention and was almost immediately termed the "mystery ship" in newspaper headlines across the country. It would continue to be a mystery for almost a week after the storm as a number of marine experts, each with their own theories as to which of the missing boats might be the one that had "turned turtle" in Lake Huron, visited the partially submerged hull, took measurements and estimates of size and shape, and announced with certainty the identity of the "mystery ship." One group argued that the boat was the *Wexford*. Another was just as positive it was the *Regina*. Still another was absolutely convinced it was the *Carruthers*.

It would finally take a diver to come out to the wreck and make an underwater investigation to determine exactly which boat it was.

Reports were coming in with frightening speed now with news of a number of vessels which had "disappeared" or failed to arrive at their scheduled ports of call. As November moved through the tenth and then the eleventh and the twelfth, the full impact of what had happened on the bellicose waters of the Great Lakes began to be known. The public was at first shocked and then appalled at the loss of men and vessels.

The *Argus* was missing. So was the *Wexford* and the *Hydrus*, the *Carruthers*, the *Price*, the *Regina*, the *McGean*, and the *Scott*. To be sure, others were at first reported as missing only to show up later, either limping in to a safe harbor or found driven on the ground somewhere along the shoreline of Lake Huron.

Reports of other vessels on other Great Lakes that were unaccounted for found their way onto the pages of the newspapers: the *Leafield* and the *Smith* missing on Lake Superior, the *Plymouth* on Lake Michigan, and the *Lightship Number 82* on Lake Erie.

Families of men aboard the missing vessels at first held out hope that the boats would be found and their loved ones would be alive. Still, the mounting concern caused a flood of inquiries at the ship owners' offices and marine terminals. There were so many calls that the November 11 edition of the Duluth *Herald* carried the following item below a headline that read:

NO USE PHONING;
NO INFORMATION
With the lightest port list of the present season and with various dire rumors of the fate of various vessels whose whereabouts are unknown at the present time, the office of the Union Tow-

ing Company has been besieged during the past twenty-four hours by hundreds of people in quest of information regarding various members of crews and missing vessels.

In answer to all this questioning those in charge of the tug office have been obliged to reply that there is absolutely no definite information that has reached the tug office, and that absolutely nothing can be affirmed or denied of the many rumors regarding the fate of some of the boats that have been out in the storm.

In the meantime public attention was being drawn to a small stretch of Canadian shoreline where graphic evidence of the magnitude of loss in the storm was floating in. Pieces of wreckage, life preservers, life rafts, and lifeboats from the *Regina*, the *Wexford*, the *Charles S. Price*, the *Isaac M. Scott*, the *James C. Carruthers*, the *John A. McGean*, the *Argus*, and the *Hydrus* were being found from Southampton south to Kettle Point and Port Franks.

And then came the grisly news that bodies were washing up on shore. The first of the dead to arrive was discovered by Robert Turnbull, a farmer who was inspecting the shoreline of his property near St. Joseph on Tuesday. The storm had largely abated and the difference between air and water temperatures resulted in a thick blanket of fog along the coastline. As he watched, Turnbull saw coming out of the fog a few hundred yards out in the lake a man whose upraised arms seemed to be waving to him. It was James Glenn, the homesick Scot from the *Wexford*. His arms were frozen stiff, his body held up by a life belt. Bobbing in the water, the outstretched arms appeared to be waving.

Following Glenn came his shipmates: Second Mate Archibald Brooks; Chief Engineer James Scott; Assistant Engineer Richard Lougheed; Allan Dodson, the watchman; and passengers Murdoch McDonald and his cousin Donald. In addition, one of the *Wexford's* lifeboats drifted in. It was empty.

Five miles south of Goderich, a life raft bearing the name *John A. McGean* drifted on to the beach. There were three bodies lashed to it, the bodies of wheelsmen George L. Smith and Thomas Stone—the two Indians from Sarnia—and John Owen, a watchman on the *McGean.*

Singly and by twos and threes they drifted in, as if coming to be present at some ghastly muster, shrouded in life jackets bearing the names of ships gone missing. The *Wexford, Argus, McGean, Hydrus, Scott, Regina, Car-ruthers,* and *Price* had all sent representatives to shore to announce to everyone that they had foundered, that their crews were all dead. Stiff, bloated, and battered, their heads capped in ice, they floated in, rolled and pitched by the combers crashing on the beach.

They came draped over life preservers, they came wrapped in each other's arms, they came frozen together in clusters. All week long they came, to be collected by area farmers who sometimes had to dig half-buried bodies out of the sand that was trying to cover them. They loaded the corpses on horse-drawn wagons and drove through snow-clogged roads to small villages where, in combination furniture store-funeral homes, they were stretched out on the floor and covered with blankets to await friends or relatives to come and claim them.

As the body wagons rolled through the village streets pedestrians stopped, the men removing their hats and the women bowing their heads in respect and mourning for the tragic loss of the sailors.

Several miles south of where the bodies from the *Wexford* had made landfall, ten men from the steamer *Regina* drifted in, some being washed ashore and some floating in the surf amid acres of cans, boxes, barrels, crates, some drums, and a large quantity of baled hay.

Moored on the beach was a *Regina* lifeboat. Inside were the frozen bodies of oiler Dave Lawson and Gustave Oleson, a fireman.

Search parties were organized to patrol the Canadian shoreline in search of bodies, and they found them. A total of fifty-six men and women tumbled on to the beaches.

In the panic and pandemonium attending the sinking of the steamer *Argus*, there apparently was time for gentle, considerate acts of chivalry. When the body of Emily Walker, the boat's cook and wife of steward William Walker, came ashore it was wearing a life preserver on which was stenciled "Captain" and a heavy coat that belonged to Chief Engineer George Zanger. When Captain Gutch's body came in it was without a life jacket.

Other members of the *Argus* crew drifted in. First Mate Van B. Young, Boatswain Mate Thomas Nelson, handyman George Hayes, oiler William LaMere, porter Leo Gardner, and wheelsman John McDonald all collected on the beach in close proximity.

Not far away lay the body of Second Mate Robert Rowan. It was ironic that Rowan should come ashore at that point. Rowan, the son of a boat captain, had been born in Kincardine, Ontario, and left to move to Conneaut, Ohio, a few years earlier to be near Cleveland, the home port of his employers. Now he had returned in a manner no one expected or wanted. His body was found a short distance from his family's property on the lakeshore. His attire at the time of his return would demonstrate that Rowan had achieved a degree of financial success during his years away from his boyhood home. He was not wearing a life jacket but was dressed in an expensive overcoat, gloves, and new overshoes.

Some of the bodies making their way to shore quite probably were never recovered. They had the additional misfortune of washing up on the rocky beaches of the Saugeen Indian Reservation. Because of the Saugeen taboo against touching the dead, the bodies were simply left where they landed until the waves returned and eventually took them back into the lake.

Later, however, the Lake Carrier's Association offered twenty-five dollars for each body that was recovered. This did much to overcome whatever reluctance may have been present, but by then it was too late to recover many of the bodies.

Within a day or two after the dead were discovered washing up on the Canadian shoreline, another grisly discovery was made.

A farmer living near Thedford, Ontario, was strolling the beaches near his property when he came upon a group of men, their arms loaded with as much of the debris laying on shore as they could carry. According to the farmer, the men had cases of canned goods, clothing, life preservers, and other items. One man had a box of cigars and another a case of one thousand lead pencils.

The farmer notified the local constable, who quickly rushed to the beach area accompanied by a Sarnia police detective and a provincial inspector of wrecks.

They encountered wagons loaded with various canned goods and other items from the missing ships. Further investigation revealed that in several places along the shore others were busily engaged in systematically looting not only the "salvage" coming in from the wrecked boats but from the dead bodies as well.

It was discovered that at least one money belt containing eight hundred dollars was taken from one of the bodies. The other bodies revealed that their pockets had been carefully emptied and valuables found were taken by the robbers.

In one instance the robberies were confirmed when it was discovered that bodies lying on one side of a wide creek that emptied into Lake Huron were found to have nothing of value on their persons while on the opposite side of the creek all of the bodies were found to have cash and other valuable possessions in their pockets.

An announcement was rapidly circulated throughout the area that anyone found in possession of articles belonging to dead sailors would be subject to a heavy fine and as much as three years in prison. Those having taken anything from the beaches were urged to return them to the place from which they had been taken.

Meanwhile, a change in wind and water-current patterns was taking many bodies out to the center of the lake, never to be found.

A few of the *Hydrus*'s crew came in. A lifeboat bearing the remains of five of the boat's crew members drifted to the beach near Kincardine, and Leslie and Kernol Christy were among them. Even in death the brothers had stuck together.

Alerted that bodies were being found on the Canadian shore, scores of people—friends, family, and company officials—flocked to the tiny villages of Thedford, Kincardine, and Goderich to walk slowly through the temporary morgues, gazing on faces, searching for a loved one or a shipmate or an employee.

Evelyn Mackley came, searching for the earthly remains of her husband, Howard, second mate on board the *Price*. She could not find him.

In Kincardine, Dickenson Christy, of Marine City, Michigan, bent with age and supported by his son Earl, identified the bodies of his two sons Kernol and Leslie, who had gone down with the *Hydrus*.

James McCutcheon, the *Wexford*'s first mate, who had been late reaching Port Huron to catch the boat, came to identify his dead comrades. With a voice trembling with emotion he admitted that twice before in his career he had missed his boat's departure and in each previous instance disaster had struck. The first time his boat had caught fire and burned with a large number of crewmen perishing. The second time his boat had been wrecked, again with a number of fatalities.

"I'm the luckiest guy alive," he said in almost a whisper.

It soon became obvious that Canada had lost the *Carruthers*, her newest and largest freighter. The evidence mounted slowly at first: a couple of oars with the boat's name printed on them, some wood paneling, a lone life preserver. Then the tug *Logie*, searching between Kincardine and Goderich, encountered miles of wreckage and debris from the missing boat, including rudders from two lifeboats, window frames, oars, and life preservers.

Later, around Point Clark, south of Kincardine, the bodies of some of the *Carruthers*'s crew began arriving on shore: Captain William Wright, identified by his magnificent red moustache and a ring bearing the initials "W.H.W."; Chief Engineer Edward O'Dell; and Mrs. Mary Agnes Heary, the cook, who would celebrate her thirty-ninth birthday in Brophey's Undertaking Parlor in Goderich.

William C. Lediard, the *Carruthers*'s first mate, had not been as easy to identify. Since he had recently shaved his own moustache, some who knew him with the facial hair were uncertain if he was who they believed. His father Edgar was brought from Toronto to view the body.

"That's Bill," the old man said, his voice quivering. "Bill shaved off his moustache when he was home in Midland a week ago last Sunday. Until now I have not seen him clean-shaven for ten years. But this is poor Bill. I'm sure of it."

It had been a tragic year for the Lediard family: Bill's death was the third in the family since January.

In Owen Sound, north of Kincardine, Mrs. William Buckley had rushed to the home of her close friend Mrs.

Richard Lougheed, wife of the second engineer aboard the
Wexford, to give whatever comfort she was capable of
providing to the woman who had just lost her husband.
Almost immediately after returning to her home, Alma
Buckley learned that her own husband William, second
engineer on the *Carruthers*, had also been reported lost.

There were scores of frightened men and women
whose loved ones had been—or were believed to have
been—out on the lakes during the worst storm to ever
strike them. They waited, with varying degrees of patience, for the newspaper reports to tell them of the fate of
their sons or daughters, husbands, brothers, sisters or
sweethearts. In some instances poignant dramas were
acted out as terrified people sought to learn about those
who had been caught in the storm.

In Sombra, Ontario, a man bent with age timidly
approached the local newspaper's managing editor and
softly inquired about his son, a member of the *Henry B.
Smith*'s crew.

"Do you think there's a bare chance my boy may be
alive," he asked, trying to control his tears. "I just can't tell
his mother that he's gone. It would plain kill her."

Milton Smith, the assistant engineer whose premonition had driven him from the *Charles S. Price*, had been
asked by the shipowners to go to Canada and attempt to
identify dead members of the crew.

In Goderich, walking slowly down the lines of bodies
stretched out on the floor of William Brophey's funeral
parlor, Smith sadly picked out his former crew members.

"That's Herbert Jones, the steward," Smith told a
constable accompanying him down the lines. "There he is
lying there with his apron still on just as if he was about to
prepare a meal, just like I saw him hundreds of times. He
must not have had time to look out for his wife's welfare.
The boat must have gone down awful quick."

Next he found Arz McIntosh. "Poor old Arz," he said

after giving the officer the wheelsman's full name. "I can see him now when he came up to me to ask if I was really leaving the boat. I'm especially sorry for poor Arz."

Next came Chief Engineer John Groundwater, who had argued so forcefully against Smith's leaving the boat before the end of the season.

"That's him. Big, good-natured John Groundwater. How the boys all liked him."

The constable was puzzled.

"Are you sure that's John Groundwater from the *Price*?" he wanted to know.

"As sure as I know my own name," Smith replied.

The constable shook his head in disbelief.

"Then why did this man have a *Regina* life jacket wrapped around him?"

The mystery made sensational news copy and spawned a rash of theories as to how a member of the *Charles S. Price* could have washed ashore wearing a life jacket from the *Regina*.

One of the most popular scenarios had the *Price* colliding with the *Regina* at some point in the storm and had at least some of the *Price*'s crew scrambling aboard the *Regina* only to have the *Regina* foundering later, at which time the *Price*'s crew donned life jackets from the *Regina*. Another theory had the *Regina* come upon the *Price*'s crewmen struggling in the water immediately after the *Price* went down. Unable to stop to pick them up, the men on the *Regina* threw life jackets to the men in the water.

To buttress their stories, newspaper reports had a number of *Price* crewmen coming ashore with the jackets from the *Regina*. However, the only documented case of someone from the *Price* wearing a *Regina* life jacket was the case of John Groundwater. And even this report has some flaws. There is a question as to whether Groundwater was actually *wearing* the life jacket. There were those who suggested that the life jacket may simply have been found lying on the sailor's body. Among the items taken by the looters were life jackets. When the threat of fine and/or imprisonment was circulated, some suggested that the looter returned and simply tossed the *Regina* life jacket on a body—that of John Groundwater.

Still, the constable's question would continue to haunt scholars and researchers. To date there has never been a totally satisfactory answer.

The magnitude of the losses in the terrible storm prompted one newspaper to editorialize:

"While the exact numbers of lost ships and crews are not yet known there can be no doubt that a terrible price has been paid."

CHAPTER 20

"It's Just Like You to Attend Your Own Wake"

ON TUESDAY, NOVEMBER 11, THOMAS THOMPSON of Hamilton, Ontario, was horrified at a telegram he had received from his daughter, Mrs. Edward Ward of Sarnia.

"JOHN HAS BEEN DROWNED. COME AT ONCE," it read.

The daughter had seen reports in the local newspaper of an unidentified member of the lost freighter *James C. Carruthers* who bore a tattoo with the initials "J.T." John Thompson was her twenty-eight-year-old brother, who sometimes worked the lake boats as a fireman. He had his initials tattooed on his arm. In addition, she knew that John had recently taken a berth aboard the *Carruthers*. She was certain that the unidentified body in Goderich was that of her brother.

Tuesday night, an exhausted and emotionally drained Thomas Thompson appeared at the Brophey funeral home and asked to view the body of the seaman with the "J.T." tattoo.

The body had been terribly battered before being recovered, but the facial features, similar to John Thompson's, were still largely recognizable. There were other similarities between the corpse stretched out on the floor and those of Thomas Thompson's son John: A deformity in the feet that caused the big toes to cross over the second digits was present. The initials "J.T." were on the body's left forearm, the same location as John Thompson's tattoo. A scar on the nose of the body was identical to one John bore, and the body's teeth had an eyetooth and two bottom teeth missing, just as Thompson did. Finally, a burn scar on the shin of one of the legs matched exactly a scar John had.

The only feature of the body that didn't match John Thompson was the hair color. John had very dark, almost black, hair while the corpse had light-brown hair. The undertaker explained that immersion in cold lake water could cause this difference, and in light of the remarkable similarities, Thomas Thompson was convinced that he had found the body of his beloved son.

Arrangements were made to have the body prepared for burial and tenderly brought to Hamilton. An expensive casket was purchased and on November 18 the casket was placed in the parlor of the family home. A cascade of floral tributes arrived and townspeople flocked to the Thompson home to participate in a wake.

One of the chief mourners of John Thompson was James Duffy, proprietor of the Northern Hotel, a local pub.

On Wednesday afternoon, as Duffy stood behind the bar of his establishment, a young man entered and ordered a beer. Duffy paled and collapsed on the floor: he had seen a ghost. Standing before him was John Thompson, the man supposedly lying in a casket in the Thompson parlor.

From the Northern, Thompson went to the family residence on North John Street, where he walked up on the porch and knocked on the front door. The house was filled with friends and relatives come to pay their respects to the drowned sailor.

Thomas answered the knock, gazed at the face of his dead son, and promptly fainted. The commotion attracted the attention of John's mother, who came to see what had happened only to fall unconscious to the floor herself.

The mourners looked with disbelief on the young man standing just inside the front door and then on the body lying in the casket. The resemblance was uncanny.

Mrs. Thompson was so overcome with emotion that she had to be put to bed under a doctor's care. Thomas Thompson, once he got over the shock of seeing that the son he believed to be dead was very much alive, considered the full import of what had happened. He had mistakenly identified as his own the body of another man's son, he had gone to great expense in the purchase of a coffin and the selection of a burial plot, and had arranged with the Reverend Father J. F. Hinchey to conduct the funeral mass. He felt embarrassed at having so many friends and relatives shocked and saddened because of his mistake. And then to have his "resurrected" son come strolling in in the middle of the wake had the old man feeling a twinge of annoyance with his son mixed in with the great joy and relief at finding him alive.

"It's just like you to come back to attend your own wake," he growled.

John, once all the tumult that greeted his surprise return had died away, explained that he had left the *Carruthers* to ship out aboard the *Maple*. He had left that ship in Welland and proceeded to Montreal, hoping to ship out on a large freighter. Because of the storm John went to Toronto, intending to come home for a few days until the weather moderated. It was there that he read a newspaper account of his "death."

Asked why he hadn't sent word immediately that he was alive, the thoughtless young man replied, "I thought it would be a really good joke to just walk in."

The misidentified body was sent back to Goderich, where along with four other bodies that could not be identified, it was tenderly buried in Maitland Cemetery east of the town.

A memorial service was held for the five on November 16 in Knox Presbyterian Church. Seventeen hundred, crowded wall-to-wall, came to hear the church choir assisted by the choirs of all the other churches in town. The Reverend J. B. Totheringhan, rector of St. George's Anglican Church of Goderich, preached the sermon. The Odd Fellows, Masons, Foresters, Orangemen, and Sons of Scotland—plus the full town council—all attended.

Following the service a parade of five glass-enclosed, horse-drawn hearses—flanked on either side by an honor guard composed of the elite of the town and preceded by a fifteen-piece band—moved slowly around the octagonal Court House Square, which was lined on both sides of the wide thoroughfare by hundreds of silent, respectful men and women.

The five men, known only to God, were initially buried side by side in separate graves, each with a simple headstone on which had been carved the name *Carruthers* and a number one through five.

Later the five were combined in a single grave capped with an imposing monument which says:

IN MEMORY OF THE UNIDENTIFIED SEAMEN
LOST IN THE GREAT LAKES DISASTER OF
NOV. 1913

Below, in large raised letters, is the simple legend:

SAILORS

Those bodies that were identified were transported for burial to their homes. John Groundwater went to Cleveland; Arz McIntosh to St. Clair, Michigan; David Lawson to Chatham, New Brunswick; and Wilson McInnes to Owen Sound, Ontario. . . .

All together, fifty-six bodies were recovered from the Canadian beaches. One additional corpse would be found the following year on the Michigan side of Lake Huron. Captain Ed McConkey from the *Regina* would make the shore near Port Sanilac.

There were many funerals held in the days immediately after the storm, majestic services in the huge cathedrals in large cities. But the most meaningful and perhaps the most touching were conducted in dozens of small chapels in small villages and towns.

Collingwood, Ontario, was just such a community. It had been devastated by a terrible, personal loss and was deep in mourning for the sons who were drowned in the vicious lakes.

On November 15, the Saturday following the storm, the town literally closed down. All businesses were closed, and flags flew at half-mast. A public demonstration of grief had to be canceled because of a smallpox epidemic raging in the town, closing the churches, schools, and theaters. Any private party or public gathering was prohibited.

Small, dignified services were held with processions to the cemetery. There was a funeral and procession for Orrin Gordon, a wheelsman on the *Wexford*. But unfortunately, his mother, Mrs. Charles Gordon, was quarantined in the hospital and couldn't attend. The funeral cortege, in deference to the ailing woman, came past her window, giving her the opportunity to wave a tearful farewell.

One particularly poignant service was held at the Indian Reserve Cemetery near the banks of the St. Clair River, south of Sarnia. The earthly remains of George L. Smith and Thomas Stone were being committed to the ground.

Approximately three hundred mourners gathered

around the open graves as Nicholas Plain spoke the eulogies. He spoke of the treacherous character of the big lakes and of the wind spirits that occasionally bring down evil storms and rob the tribes of good and decent men.

Just as the service finished, from out on the river a half mile away came the long, low, mournful moan of a steamer's whistle, almost as if in a conscious salute to two sailors who had perished in a ship gone missing.

CHAPTER 21

"It's the Price"

THE PEOPLE OF TWO NATIONS—the United States and Canada—reeled in disbelief at the frightful cost in human life taken in one double-barreled, savage storm on the Great Lakes.

As the casualty rate mounted day upon day, the full impact of what had happened in five days seemed beyond reason. Hundreds of men and women had been taken by the violent lakes to die in the most grisly and appalling fashion. They had been sucked beneath the thundering waves or had floated upon them until the numbing cold had drained the life out of them, leaving them to bob on the surface like so much refuse—flotsam—to be eventually washed ashore, there to be battered by the rocks until their faces were barely recognizable. And then they were loaded on horse carts like cords of firewood, taken to strange places and stretched out on cold, hard floors until some loved one might be found and brought to the place to identify and claim what was left.

The very thought of the ghastly tableau being acted out in several Canadian villages was incomprehensible to those who were forced to witness or participate in the macabre ritual.

Efforts were increased to find and recover every one of the bodies of the lost mariners. The Lake Carrier's

133

Association had urged a thorough land and sea search for the dead along the shores of Lake Huron and Lake Superior, with the help of the Government Revenue Service (later the IRS), which patrolled the Great Lakes prior to the Coast Guard. The Michigan state game warden, William Oates, was one official approached for assistance. A wire from the association's William Livingstone petitioned Oates for help:

> YOU ARE AWARE OF GREAT LOSS OF LIFE IN THE TERRIBLE STORM WHICH SWEPT THE GREAT LAKES LAST WEEK STOP WE ARE HAVING CONSIDERABLE DIFFICULTY IN RECOVERING BODIES OF SAILORS WHO WERE LOST STOP
>
> THIS BEING YOUR HUNTING SEASON WITH YOUR GAME WARDENS PATROLLING THE FORESTS AND SHORES TO SEE THAT GAME LAWS ARE OBSERVED BY HUNTERS AS A MATTER OF PUBLIC INTEREST IN HUMANITY WILL YOU NOT KINDLY INSTRUCT THEM AND ALSO HAVE THEM ASK HUNTERS TO CAREFULLY EXAMINE THE LAKE SHORE WHEN HUNTING IN THAT VICINITY AND PROMPTLY REPORT THEIR FINDINGS STOP
>
> IT WOULD RELIEVE MANY SORROWING HEARTS AND WE WOULD APPRECIATE IT MORE THAN WORDS CAN EXPRESS STOP

The Michigan game wardens were immediately instructed to carry out the request of the Lake Carrier's Association.

To some extent the public's attention was diverted by the "mystery ship" that continued to float, bottom-side up, just north of Port Huron. The thirst to know what ship it was became unbearable.

Finally, as the seas calmed sufficiently to permit a

diver to go down to the wreck and make a positive identification, Livingstone ordered an investigation of the derelict. "For God's sake, send someone out there and send me
the bill," he insisted.

On November 15, William H. Baker, donning a cum-
bersome diving suit, prepared to slip over the side of the
tug *Sport.*

"We laid near the wreck all night waiting for the
dawn," Baker said later. "We had everything arranged to
make the descent at the earliest possible moment."

Baker had been chosen for the dive because he was
considered by the owner of the tug, Captain Robert B.
Thompson, to be the best diver on the lakes. Peter Bachus,
one of the most expert diver's assistants, was brought
along to tend to Baker.

At six that morning, Baker was lowered over the stern
of the tug, which had been positioned close to the bow of
the mystery boat.

"As I started down I felt her sides for twenty feet,"
Baker stated later. "Then I lost her again. I started up
again and I ran into the pipe rail around her Texas work.
I hung on there until I found out where I was at. Then I
went down that pipe rail until I ran into the bulwarks of
the wreck. The bulwarks were painted white. There was a
round railing on the edge of the bulwarks and I went
around that railing until I ran across her name."

In the murky twilight below the surface of the lake,
Baker had to practically push his face against the letters
on the boat's bow to see them. The name, as was the boat,
was upside down. He silently spelled them out one letter at
a time until he had the name.

"Her full name is there. I read the name over twice to
be absolutely positive. The name is painted in black letters
on white bulwarks."

Once he had what he'd been sent down for, Baker,

pulling himself along the side, holding tight to the railing
to prevent being carried off by the strong current, moved
forward to the boat's stem, looking for evidence of a
collision or other signs of damaged plates. He came upon
two rows of portholes, all of which were secured with the
glass unbroken. The curtain in one was hanging out,
apparently caught when the porthole was closed and fastened.

Baker investigated about forty-eight feet of the forward section of the boat. He noticed that the bow was
being held up by air trapped inside: he could see two
streams of bubbles coming from the hull. He attempted to
get inside the boat but the water currents began to toss
him around dangerously. He signaled to be pulled back to
the surface. He'd been down about an hour.

The men on the tug's deck waited anxiously as the
diver was hoisted aboard and the huge metal diving helmet
was removed. What was the name of the "mystery" boat?

"It's the *Price*," he said.

Area newspapers announced in huge headlines the
name everyone had puzzled over for nearly a week.

Immediately, there were new theories advanced: The
Price had indeed collided with the *Regina*, which would
certainly be located nearby. The *Regina* was probably
directly underneath the *Price*, holding her partially on the
surface. Most of the crew would probably be found inside
the wreck, certainly the men who had been working in the
engine room would be found there. The *Price* would be
refloated, put upright, and placed back in service.

The experts were wrong on each count. The *Regina*
was not found nearby, and it definitely was not beneath
the *Price*. And the *Price* would not be refloated and put
upright, although attempts were made to pump air inside
the hull to displace the lake water. But these efforts failed
and the *Charles S. Price* slowly settled to the bottom,
where it remains today.

The *Regina* was finally found seventy-three years after the savage night when she disappeared. She was not near the *Price* but almost twenty miles north of where the *Price* overturned.

In addition to the *Price* and *Regina*, four other boats that sank in the same storm have been found, three in Lake Huron and one in Lake Erie. The *Lightship Number 82* washed ashore near Buffalo the year after the storm and was refitted and returned to service. In 1971 scuba diver Kent Bellrichard came upon the wreck of the *Isaac M. Scott* nine miles northeast of Thunder Bay Island. Like the *Price*, she is overturned, lying in the mud 200 feet below the surface. The *Argus* was discovered the following year by diver Dick Race, also bottom-up and lying in 250 feet of water about thirteen miles north of Pointe Aux Barques. Not far from the *Argus*, ten miles off Port Hope, lies the *John A. McGean*, located in 1985 by diver/photographer Dave Trotter in 175 feet of water, also upside down.

Of the twelve vessels to sink in the storm of November 7–11, 1913, six have never been found. The barge *Plymouth* and the steamers *Henry B. Smith*, *Leafield*, *James C. Carruthers*, *Wexford*, and *Hydrus* are still considered ships gone missing.

CHAPTER 22

"Who Is to Blame?"

TWELVE BOATS HAD SUNK. Another twenty-five had been driven on the rocks, and many of these were considered "constructive losses," or total wrecks.

Between 250 and 300 men and women had drowned or frozen to death in the water. The exact number is not known due to the often careless record-keeping of the shipping companies and the laxity of the rules, which permitted those who knew the captain or an influential crew member to "hitch a ride" on one of the freighters and never appear on any manifest or passenger list.

The cost to shipowners was in the millions, which in 1913 was a staggering sum. The disruption of trade on the world's busiest commercial waterway was devastating.

Once the numbness of the terrible tragedy had worn off, the cry for an explanation was taken up. "Who is to blame?" was an oft-repeated question. The Canadian shipping companies had decided, even before the recovered bodies were all in the ground, that they would not be held responsible. "No Compensation for Loss of Sailors" read one newspaper headline, while another said, "An Act of God Will Be Defense of Shipowners."

To its credit, the Lake Carrier's Association agreed to pay on the welfare plan established with its membership. The beneficiaries of the 153 who died on Lake Carrier's

Association boats were paid a total of $17,825. Compensation for a sailor's death depended on the position he held aboard the steamers. The highest amounts went to the survivors of shipmasters. The wife of Captain Paul Gutch of the *Argus* received $500. A first mate was worth $250, while a chief engineer brought $400. A first assistant engineer was considered of equal value as a first mate—$250. A steward or a second mate or assistant engineer had a death value of $150. In the $100 class came wheelsmen, firemen, oilers, watchmen, and handymen. Bringing up the rear at $75 were second cooks, porters, deckhands, and ordinary seamen.

While in 1913 an entire men's wardrobe could be purchased for $25, a good meal for a quarter, and a banquet for a dollar, $75 to comfort and sustain the family of a deckhand was woefully parsimonious.

A want ad in the *Detroit Free Press* of November 2, 1913, invited applications for the positions of a licensed engineer and assistant engineer for a "light vessel," offering $600 to $800 a year.

In Canada, where the shipowners wanted no part in compensating its lost seamen, a relief fund was established asking for contributions from business and private sources. Over $100,000 was collected within two weeks.

The U.S. and Canadian weather bureaus came under bitter attack by shipowners and shipmasters.

Captain Frank C. Pratt of the steamer *James C. Dunham* was among the first to raise his voice in criticism of the warnings that were given as the storm approached.

"The United States Weather Bureau itself is responsible for the loss of life and property in the storm," Pratt insisted. "The forecasts were not only inadequate but are responsible [for the losses]. No warning was given us along the lakes and we did not know there would be a storm."

Pratt claimed that while in Duluth on Friday night, November 7, he noticed his barometer was low and called the Duluth weather bureau, which informed him that there would be a strong northwest wind and a heavy snowfall. He took this to mean that conditions on the lake would be well within the capabilities of his boat and sailed out of the harbor.

"There was no warning of a storm," Pratt went on. "And not only that, but the forecast given was absolutely unreliable. The wind switched after I had been out for a short time and came in the opposite direction from that which I had been told."

Other mariners agreed, claiming that weather forecasters appeared to see nothing more ominous that weekend than high winds, a few snow flurries and a drop in temperature."

On Saturday afternoon the forecast issued for the upper Great Lakes until 7:00 Sunday night called for "high west and northwest winds; snow flurries and colder tonight."

Included was a "storm warning" such as was routinely supplied for any unusually high-wind forecasts. No hurricane warnings were provided.

In no case, the ship captains asserted, were storm signals displayed as they should have been, and the forecasts that were received gave little indication of the hurricane-force winds that were to sweep down on the lakes.

The captains further pointed to the forecast issued on Saturday for Sunday, November 9:

"For upper lakes: High west and northwest winds *diminishing* tonight on west Superior. Snow flurries and colder tonight: Sunday *generally fair.*"

The irate captains argued that "extra precautions should have been taken by the weather bureaus to inform the men of the coming gale."

At least one congressman had joined the public outcry against the U.S. Weather Bureau. Congressman William Gorden of Ohio's twentieth district—the district in which the Ohio shipping executives were constituents—wired President Woodrow Wilson demanding a full investigation by Secretary of Agriculture David F. Houston, head of the department having responsibility for the weather bureau.

The weather bureau, attempting to head off being made a scapegoat for the ghastly results of a rare and totally unpredictable meteorological aberration, was quick to respond.

Houston produced Chief Forecaster Harry C. Frankenfield and Professor Charles E. Marvin, chief of the weather bureau, who publicly discussed the matter thoroughly, offering as evidence weather maps, reports, and proof of the signals being displayed before and during the storm. Secretary Houston explained in detail the birth and growth of the killer storm and the warnings that were hoisted beginning on Thursday, November 6.

"The department will refuse absolutely to take any responsibility for the acts of vessel owners or captains in ignoring the plain warnings shown by the records to have been issued in advance of the storm," Houston trumpeted. "We are not going to submit to any effort on the part of vessel owners or other interests to make a 'goat' out of any of the weather forecasters along the Great Lakes."

In response to published charges that the weather bureau had given inadequate warning to shipping companies on the Great Lakes of the approach of a terrible storm, the records submitted by Houston demonstrated that storm warnings had been raised at 113 points around the Great Lakes, including nineteen weather-bureau installations from which comprehensive data regarding the potential bad weather could have been gotten upon request.

As the forecaster at the weather bureau's administrative headquarters for most of the Great Lakes, William H. Alexander felt obliged to respond to the criticism he was receiving from the Cleveland-based shipmasters.

Alexander argued that he acted promptly in ordering the raising of storm warnings as soon as the information from Washington was received. Alexander also claimed that efforts he had made in the past to notify the managers of shipping companies of weather changes had been met with marked ambivalence and the impression that he was stepping out of line.

"The attitude of the vessel owners," he once remarked to a colleague, "has been such that we felt we were bothering the officials of these companies."

In response to a reporter's question as to whether the companies had ever called him for weather information, he replied, "Only the passenger lines and the Pennsylvania & Ohio Transportation Company, operators of the car ferry *Ashtabula*, have seemed to appreciate this service and call us daily."

And Secretary Houston was not yet finished with his assault on the shipping companies.

"The history of the Great Lakes," he proclaimed, "contains many instances of storm warnings having been ignored by vessel owners. And in many cases the vessel owners taking these risks have gotten out without a loss. In cases where they take the hazard and lose, they themselves must assume responsibility."

In an example of overkill, the bureau issued a lengthy report on the "Climatological Data for November, 1913, District No. 4, the Lake Region." It was authored by J. H. Armington, acting district editor for the monthly *Weather Review*. The report began:

The storm of the 7th to 10th was one of the severest that has ever crossed the Lake Region.

While higher winds have been recorded in connection with other disturbances, the velocities experienced in this storm were at most stations far above the verifying limits for windstorms, and then continued so long as to cause extraordinarily high seas which swept the Lakes with tremendous force. Many disasters and casualties occurred as a result of the storm. Breakwaters were broken up, and banks on the windward shore were badly washed out. The disturbance was accompanied over the central and eastern portions of the lakes by driving snow, which increased the precarious situation of vessels, tied up land traffic, and caused much damage to a considerable distance from the shore.

The report went on to explain that "owing to the exceptional severity of this storm," the various weather-reporting stations went to great detail in reporting the data.

The report described the conditions in Duluth, Minnesota, by stating that there was "no loss of life or vessel property on the extreme western end of Lake Superior as a result of the great storm which passed over the lake region on the 7th to 10th, but some local damage occurred to property ashore in sections near Duluth-Superior harbor during the northwest gale which prevailed on the afternoon of the 7th."

It stated that during this storm, the maximum wind velocities ranged anywhere from thirty-four to sixty-two miles an hour between 1:00 P.M. and 7:00 P.M., its intensity being greatest about 7:00 P.M. and ceasing abruptly a few minutes after seven o'clock that evening. The report indicated that "this was the only blow of consequence during the month."

In Sault Ste. Marie, the report said, the "storm of the

7th to 10th was the most severe experienced on the lakes
for many years. A large fleet anchored in the upper river
and the lower part of Whitefish Bay. The wind and seas
sweeping down the bay, into the river, caused the steamers *J. C. Hutchinson* and *Fred G. Hartwell* to drag their
anchors and strike rock shoals, sinking both vessels and
causing heavy damage."

The report went on to say that the steamer *William
Nottingham* struck a shoal near Whitefish Point and was
"very badly damaged." Three of her crew were drowned
when they attempted to lower a lifeboat to make their way
to shore and summon help. Also according to the report
the steamer *Cornell* was caught in the "gale" above Whitefish Point from Friday morning until Monday night, sus-
taining heavy damage, and kept off the beach "only with
the greatest difficulty."

On November 9, the wind at Sault Ste. Marie, the
report continued, reached a maximum velocity at 6:00
P.M. of only thirty-seven miles an hour from the northwest,
while out on the lakes, ship captains were experiencing
sixty- to eighty-mile-an-hour winds.

Citing Captain John Noble of the steamer *Cornell*,
the report described a "very peculiar feature." About
midnight on November 6, while on a course from Whitefish Point to Keweenaw and about fifty miles west of the
point with the wind light from the southeast, "he suddenly
encountered an unusually high northwest seas, and
shortly afterward the wind backed to northerly, blowing a
gale, which lasted until Monday night."

And so it went, page after page describing what had
occurred on the lakes during the four-day storm. And
while it made for interesting reading it did very little to
settle the question of who was to blame.

In Canada the debate over who should bear the fault
for the unprecedented loss of life raged on.

The Toronto newspapers were printing many opinions stating that the shipowners, who were becoming rich from an annual profit of 20 to 30 percent, were forcing their captains and crews to sail in bad weather on unsafe vessels.

A. A. Wright, the manager of the St. Lawrence & Chicago Steam Navigation Company, owners of the *James C. Carruthers*, bitterly denounced such claims, adding, "In twenty years of conversing with men who have been sailing first class steel ships, similar to those which were lost, no master ever paid any attention to the weather reports. If they had, they would never have got anywhere, and they have always guided their actions by the weather they were experiencing and what they could judge they were likely to encounter."

Wright claimed that the responsibility for the losses belonged to the Dominion Meteorological Department.

"The weather bulletins were all wrong," he insisted, pointing to the forecast for Lake Huron and Georgian Bay for November 8 and 9: "Gales southwesterly to northwesterly; rain, turning in many localities to snow; Sunday, strong winds and gales, northwesterly, decreasing by night; local snow flurries but mostly fair and cold."

What was actually experienced on Georgian Bay on Saturday was a strong gale from the southwest that continued until 6:00 A.M. Sunday, when after a few minutes of calm the winds began to shift around to the north-northwest. "This persisted," Wright argued, "until between 11 A.M. and 12 A.M., when a furious snowstorm came on, which persevered until Monday morning. The wind continued from the north and north-northeast and blew harder than the captains of two boats which were on Georgian Bay had ever experienced, with the heaviest sea either had ever encountered."

Wright continued, "It should be very evident that in

this case the weather probabilities gave not the slightest indication either of the kind of storm or the direction from which the wind would come."

R. F. Supart, director of the Dominion Meteorological Department, disputed Wright's assertions that the forecasts were totally inaccurate, stating that the variation in the predicted wind was only an eighth of the compass—or forty-five degrees—from what the weather department had said it would be, from north-northwest to north-northeast. He further said that a hurricane warning probably should have been posted, but "the hurricane signal has not been used for over fifty years, and is now only operated in the south for the West Indies hurricanes and tropical tornadoes. We had up our No. 4 signals, our heavy gale warnings. They were hoisted at 11:00 A.M. on Friday, two days before the storm hit Lake Huron. In November this signal always meant that any vessel putting out did so at a great risk. All we could do was give the warnings."

Back in the United States a high official of the weather bureau admitted that perhaps the warning system needed improving:

> There is no question but there should be signals showing more than the usual storm is expected. At present the bureau has only two signals to flash to vessels on the Great Lakes when a storm is approaching: the small craft signal and the storm signal.
>
> The warning indicated by the small craft signal is for the smaller boats to seek shelter or take necessary precautions, and the other signal, the one which is used to warn the larger craft, is for the purpose of informing the lake maritime community that a severe storm is due, there being no suggestion as to the severity of the storm aside from the fact that there is danger.

I think everyone concerned is of the opinion that regulations should require special warnings for the particularly dangerous storms where wind and snow combine.

The maritime industry insisted that the weather bureau was responsible to provide extra means to have the lake boats notified of the coming storm and its anticipated severity, since the storm warnings that were posted were the same as those routinely hoisted for "every little blow that comes along."

Yet many sailors pointed out that the forecasts did provide the warning that there would be "high west to northwest winds," and that an experienced shipmaster should know that winds of thirty to forty miles an hour combined with snow makes for extremely dangerous conditions. The masters should have been able to determine the potential nature of the storm.

It was undisputed that the storm warnings were properly displayed. Every vessel passing Port Huron, headed into Lake Huron, or coming south through the Soo had to sail right by the signals. At the lower end of Lake Huron, the storm signals were flying on both sides of the St. Clair River—at Port Huron and at Sarnia.

What couldn't be known by either the weather bureau or the shipmasters studying the weather map was that the storm which struck Lake Huron was a rare and extremely savage combination of three weather systems that changed directions, from the northwest to northeast, so suddenly that the wind was blowing from one direction while the seas were running in a totally different one. This condition was simply not predictable, it was unprecedented in the annals of meteorological science.

Additional support in defense of the weather bureau came from among the shipmasters.

Captain C. W. Watson, skipper of the steamer *George*

F. Brownell, who had sailed through the storm on Lake Huron, stated, "I think the storm had been traveling along the regular storm track and after reaching the Great Lakes region was diverted from that track so suddenly that its deflection couldn't be noted until after the storm was upon us. The high north-northeast winds were perhaps a sort of flare back of the high southwest winds of the day previous."

Captain Watson further stated that his own forecast on November 7 was that the wind would shift from south to southwest, blowing hard from that direction for about twelve hours and then shift again, this time to the northwest, before blowing itself out after about twenty-four to thirty-six hours, "which is the usual course taken by such storms."

"There can be no question but that this was a freak storm," he continued, "which defied even the fine equipment of the weather bureau. On passing Port Huron, westerly signals were shown by both the American and Canadian weather stations.

"In view of this, I think criticism of the weather bureau is entirely unjustified. If old Mother Nature chose to depart from the usual course without advance notice, the weather bureau can hardly be held responsible."

Eagerly thrusting themselves into the fray, the newspapers offered such irresponsible suggestions as closing the shipping season early enough that "such storms could not be encountered," and "when a steel vessel simply sinks in the open lake, somebody should be indicted for manslaughter."

As is often the case, the truth lies somewhere in between two divergent opinions: there was more than enough blame to go around.

The reporting and classification of storm systems by the weather bureaus—both American and Canadian— were terribly lacking in specificity. A more comprehensive method of alerting lake boats and shipping companies of the real potential of coming storms was certainly needed. Unfortunately, it would not be forthcoming, at least not until the advent of more sophisticated electronic and scientific analytical equipment. And even then, the art of predicting short-term weather would remain elusive, purely a matter of educated guesswork.

As for the shipowners, there was sufficient evidence presented to justify many of the claims of greed and insensitivity in regard to the care taken for the safety of the crews.

There was a pervasive sense among the shipping-industry managers that getting as many cargoes delivered without delay preceded any concern for whether leaving port in times of possible bad weather was prudent and wise.

Shipmasters who were found to frequently "heave to" when the skies turned gray were summarily reprimanded and warned that retaining their commands rested heavily on how productive they were.

Although oceangoing vessels were required by law to have watertight integrity throughout the ship, lake boats were not. The cargo holds in bulk freighters were little more than barges, huge warehouses that were partitioned off with nothing more than "screen bulkheads"—wire fences to keep the cargoes from shifting fore or aft. Water getting into any cargo hold would flow unobstructed into all the others. This design flaw remains in the huge ore carriers and Great Lakes freighters of today. And it has contributed to the loss of many boats and hundreds of helpless, terrified sailors.

While the call for investigations and hearings echoed across North America following the frightful storm of November 1913—and, indeed, several were convened—nothing of substance resulted.

The boats continued to ply the dangerous waters of

the Great Lakes when the gales of November threatened, the storm signals hoisted in times of bad weather continued largely unchanged, and shipmasters continued to be pressured to move the cargo, to deliver on time, to make "just one more run" before the season ended. Vicious storms continued to prey upon the lakes, and, most sadly, boats continued to join the thousands that are scattered over the floor of the "eighth sea," taking their screaming crews with them.

On November 26, 1913, it was reported that two more bodies from the storm were washed ashore. The body of R. A. Somerville, a porter on the *Hydrus*, came ashore near Stokes Bay, Ontario. From Menominee, Michigan, came the report that a body believed to be from the barge *Plymouth* washed up on the beach of eastern Lake Michigan near Frankfort, Michigan. With these two discoveries, the search for further bodies of lost crewmen was officially terminated.

The families of nearly two hundred missing sailors would live out the remainder of their lives with the enduring uncertainty of what exactly had happened to their loved ones. Several would be haunted by the specter of lucky sailors that might very well have died were it not for strange, unexplained twists of fate: Milton Smith and John Thompson, who had left their boats on sudden whims, and Joe Henderson, who had been engineer aboard the *Argus* but who had refused to sail on her because of a union dispute.

Some would be haunted in other ways.

At the height of the storm on Sunday night, November 9, Mrs. Mary E. Young, of Marine City, Michigan, had a vision of her son, Van B. Young, first mate of the *Argus*. As she dozed in a chair, Mrs. Young dreamed of seeing her son in a lifeboat with huge waves towering over him.

"Come, mother, jump in," he shouted to her.

Mrs. Young was convinced that her boy was on the water at that precise moment. She was said to have had great difficulty accepting his death.

Others found accepting the fate of the men and women who drowned on the Great Lakes in the worst storm to ever strike them a psychological impossibility.

In Menominee, Michigan, home to the crew of the ill-fated barge *Plymouth*, at least one person suffered mental problems following the loss of the seven men of the *Plymouth*, problems he had great difficulty in dealing with.

In what was then a typical style of newspaper writing, the following insensitive account appeared in the *Detroit Free Press* December 1, 1913:

MENOMINEE, MICH. Nov. 30

Harry Elkey, twenty-one years old, is a raving maniac as the result of brooding over the loss of the barge *Plymouth*, with her crew of seven Menominee men. Elkey is now in a padded cell.

On U.S. 25 just south of Port Sanilac, Michigan, there is a small roadside park. Located on the water's edge, it affords a magnificent view of a portion of Lake Huron. Looking south at the lake, one can almost see the spot below which rests the remains of the *Regina*. Thirty-five miles to the north is the location of the wreck of the *John A. McGean*. Far out in the lake, during the shipping season, the large one-thousand-foot freighters and ore carriers can be seen slowly plowing their way through the water, their crews generally oblivious of the fact that they are moving across the graveyards of hundreds of men and women who dared to challenge the vagaries of the winds and waves that frequently visit these waters.

As a reminder to tourists visiting the small roadside park of the dangers of what many unfamiliar with the

Great Lakes think of as small placid pools, a metal plaque
has been erected by the Michigan State Historical Society.
The marker reads:

THE GREAT STORM
OF 1913
Sudden tragedy struck the
Great Lakes on November 9,
1913, when a storm whose
equal veteran sailors could
not recall left in its wake
death and destruction. The
grim toll was 235 seamen
drowned, ten ships sunk,* and
more than twenty others
driven ashore. Here on Lake
Huron all 178 crewmen on
the eight ships claimed by
its waters were lost. For
sixteen terrible hours, gales
of cyclonic fury made man
and his machines helpless.

---

*The state historians overlooked the barge *Plymouth* and *Lightship Number 82* in reporting the total number of vessels sunk
in the storm.

CHAPTER 23

An Epilogue

THE GALES OF NOVEMBER CONTINUED to take their toll, although it would be twenty-seven years before they churned up another storm on the lakes with the lethal ferocity of the great storm of 1913. The Armistice Day storm of 1940 was followed by memorable November storms in 1958, when the *Bradley* sank; in 1966, when the *Morrell* disappeared; and, perhaps most famously, in 1975, when the *Edmund Fitzgerald* went down.

THE ARMISTICE DAY STORM

The Armistice Day storm of 1940 did not claim as many lives or vessels as the 1913 storm did, but it would become well remembered in the minds of those caught on the open water for its savage fury, hurricane winds, and towering waves, and it would spark a long-lasting debate among those who had weathered each of the terrible blows as to which was truly the most fearsome.

The autumn of 1940 around Lake Michigan had been among the most pleasant in memory. Mild sun-filled days with gentle winds and little rain had helped to take the minds of most off the insanity raging in Europe and threatening to drag America's youth into the deadly conflict.

153

Sunday, November 10, was an especial bonus to the Midwesterners who seized the opportunity to spend the day in the open, taking a quiet drive in the country or a satisfying walk in the woods. Yet as the delightful weather was being savored throughout the lake region, an intense low-pressure system was even then speeding across the northern tier of states.

On November 8, the system had roared off the Pacific Ocean. Its cyclonic winds had smashed into the state of Washington, blasting into the Tacoma Narrows Bridge, causing it to sway precipitously and finally to collapse into the gorge below. The terrifying image captured on newsreel film of the thrashing structure in its death-throes earned the majestic span the disparaging sobriquet "The Galloping Bridge."

At about the same time, a separate low-pressure cell was sliding down the eastern slopes of the Rocky Mountains, pulling the hot, radiated heat from the southern Great Plains and mixing it with the moisture-laden air from the Gulf of Mexico and southern Mississippi Valley before veering northeast toward the Great Lakes.

As the two systems approached each other, there was generated a counterclockwise circulation of the warm air trapped between, developing into a gigantic storm factory that covered thousands of square miles.

As darkness cloaked Lake Michigan on the tenth, ships were pounding along in quiet seas caressed by gentle breezes.

Rounding the tip of Michigan's "mitten" Monday morning, where Lake Huron and Lake Michigan converge, the 420-foot Interlake Steamship Company bulk carrier *William B. Davock* was heading for South Chicago with a load of coal. Sixty miles astern, loaded with grain from Fort William, Ontario, on the north shore of Lake Superior, was the Canadian freighter *Anna C. Minch*, bound for Chicago.

As the *Davock* cleared Grays Reef and steered south-southwest to pass Beaver Island and set a course for the Manitou Passage, Captain Charles W. Allen commented over the radiotelephone on the beautiful, mild November weather.

At about ten o'clock that Armistice Day morning, those who were scheduled to participate in a formal parade through Chicago's Loop were beginning to assemble. There was to be silent observance precisely at 11:00 A.M., the exact moment when the World War I armistice took effect—the eleventh hour of the eleventh day of the eleventh month. This was to be followed by a few brief tributes to the fallen heroes of that war.

A similar tribute was to be held thirty-five miles southwest in Joliet, Illinois. But a sudden blast of frigid wind swept down on the waiting multitude, pelting them with hail and airborne debris and sending them fleeing for shelter. Store windows were blown in, and trees were uprooted and hurled against cars and buildings.

The storm traveled to Chicago in just fifteen minutes, where the powerful winds tore roofs from buildings and shingles flew like confetti. Chimneys crumbled and fell or exploded from the force of the sudden winds, sending bricks flying like cannon shots. A ten-story advertising sign at Randolph and the Outer Drive, costing over $175,000, was reduced to a useless pile of rubble and twisted steel in a matter of minutes.

In Gary, Indiana, a radio transmitting tower was snapped in two by the wind. The station's call letters, ironically, were WIND.

The level of Lake Michigan dropped almost five feet from the driving pressure of the storm upon the water, pushing out ever-heightening waves.

Meanwhile, out on Lake Michigan, Captain Harley O. Norton of the *New Haven Sacony* looked at the weather forecast issued at midnight and was puzzled by what he

saw. The forecast called for strong northeast winds on
November 11. But the winds were from the southeast, and
his years of experience on the lakes told him that southeast winds rarely spawn northeast gales. But since his boat
was headed for Muskegon, Michigan, and just in case the
weather prediction proved correct, Norton hauled the *New
Haven Sacony* close in to the east shore of the lake to
take advantage of the lee of the landmass. He reasoned
that he could always swing back into deeper waters if
conditions warranted.

About two hours ahead of Norton was the 253-foot
Novadoc, headed up the lake with a load of coke for Lake
Superior. Her captain, too, had opted to run in close to
the Michigan shoreline.

By early afternoon the wind had swung around and
was coming out of the southwest. Captain Norton recognized immediately what was about to happen and swung
his vessel around to port, into the wind and the storm that
was thundering down on him with black, threatening
clouds that rolled and boiled as they approached.

Captain Donald Steip of the *Novadoc*, ahead and to
the north, had been caught suddenly by the wind and
rising seas. Already close in to shore—just a few hundred
yards out—his boat was in peril.

At Ludington, Michigan, Captain A. E. Christoffersen
ordered the watch out of the Coast Guard tower, fearing
imminent collapse. It mattered little whether or not
anyone remained on duty: visibility was so poor that nothing could be seen anyway.

At about 11:00 P.M., two large car ferries, the *City of
Flint* and the *NO. 21*, attempting to dock, were having
considerable trouble. The *NO. 21* was driven against the
wharf pilings and couldn't move, and the *City of Flint*
missed the entrance piers altogether and was pushed
broadside to the beach by the force of the wind and waves.
Thirty-foot waves began to pound and batter her, forcing

her skipper to order the sea cocks opened, allowing the craft to settle to the sand bottom.

The seas exploded against her starboard side, sending spray flying in the air and over her masthead. But the *City of Flint* was able to continue making steam to provide heat and light for her forty-eight crew members and passengers.

Twenty miles to the south, at Little Sable Point, the *Novadoc* could resist the quartering seas no longer. She was hurled aground, her hull beginning to falter almost immediately. As snow and sleet lashed at her, the boat's lights blinked several times and went out for good.

William Krewell, the lighthouse keeper at Little Sable Point, observed the vessel's grounding and knew of the danger to her crew. He notified the Ludington Coast Guard station, then ran to the beach opposite the *Novadoc* and began signaling with a flashlight. He received no response from the stricken vessel.

All up and down the lake, reports were coming in of incredible waves of thirty-five feet and higher, building more quickly than even seasoned veterans of those waters could ever recall. The waves were being driven by winds that had been reported at one hundred miles per hour in some places on the lake. There were reports from a dozen locations around Lake Michigan of ships in trouble: the *Sinaloa*, with steam lines broken and no power, had been thrown against the reefs at Wisconsin's Porte Des Morts— "Death's Door"; the *Frank J. Peterson* was driven ashore on Saint Helena Island in the Straits of Mackinac; nearby, the *Conneaut* radioed that she was grounded with her bottom torn, her rudder carried away, and her propeller stripped; and the *Frank Billings* signaled that she was dangerously close to the rocks at Grays Reef with her pilot-house windows blown in, her wheelsman injured, and her forward quarters partially flooded.

To the south, the tanker *Justine C. Allen*, outbound

from Indiana Harbor, reported a broken rudder cable and was in danger of being swept around. The tankers *Mercury* and *Crudoil* and the fishing tugs *Indian* and *Richard H.* were all overdue and feared lost.

At daybreak, beach watchers south of Grand Haven, Michigan, found parts of a shattered lifeboat, oars, doors, and the top of a pilothouse, all belonging to the *New Haven Sacony*. To those retrieving the battered pieces of the vessel, there was no doubt that she had broken into a thousand parts and was scattered all over the southern end of the lake or resting somewhere on the bottom.

As a matter of fact, while the beach watchers collected rubble, the *New Haven Sacony*—at least what was left of her—was crawling toward Chicago, looking more like an iceberg than a boat. Her captain would later tell of the huge waves that rolled in seemingly endless succession over her, carrying away her lifeboats, deck gear, ventilators, and railing. A wave smashed in the pilothouse windows, carrying away the compass, lake charts, and a chair. A monster wave then took the pilothouse itself, leaving Captain Norton and the wheelsman standing there with only the wheelstand remaining. Drenched and freezing cold, they nevertheless managed to keep the vessel out of the troughs and sailing ahead.

The tankers *Crudoil* and *Mercury* both survived the storm to limp into port. Both fishing tugs, the *Indian* and the *Richard H.*, were thrown on the shore and wrecked, but their crews survived.

After thirty-six hours without food or heat, seventeen members of the *Novadoc* crew were finally rescued by the fishing tug the *Three Brothers*. The *Novadoc's* cook, Joe Shane, and his helper, Philip Flavin, had been swept overboard when they attempted to dash from the after deckhouse forward to join other members of the crew.

On Tuesday afternoon, November 12, the first bodies

from the Interlake Steamship Company's *William B. Davock* began washing ashore near Ludington. Twelve miles south, at Pentwater, Michigan, the men of the Canadian freighter *Anna C. Minch* were also coming in amid the shattered debris of furniture, cabin doors, and unused life preservers, all mixed with the swollen grain from her cargo hold.

The *Minch* had broken in two before going down about a mile south of Pentwater. The *Davock* was found in May 1972 in 204 feet of water off Big Sable Point, north of Ludington. She was upside down, her rudder hard to port, as if she had been struggling to get out of a trough but had been rolled over by one or more gigantic waves with no time to announce her plight.

A total of fifty-eight men died on the lake in the terrible blow of 1940. But as it turned out, they were not the only hapless victims of the storm.

The unseasonably mild weather before the violent tempest struck had enticed many duck hunters to the lakes and marshes in the area. Unfortunately they had come unprepared for the severe change in temperature that was to follow, dressing instead for the gentle conditions that had prevailed the previous week. Fifty of them froze to death in their blinds and small boats before they could be rescued.

"WE ARE IN SERIOUS TROUBLE"

It was November again on the lakes—November 1958—and Captain Roland Bryan, skipper of the *Carl D. Bradley*, a 640-foot bulk freighter owned by the U.S. Steel Corporation, feared that his boat was long overdue for repairs.

"The hull is not good," he confided in a letter to a friend. To another friend he said, "This boat is getting pretty ripe for too much weather. I'll be glad when they get her fixed up."

The corporation had assured their fifty-two-year-old master from Loudonville, New York, that the boat was to be fitted with a new cargo hold costing eight hundred thousand dollars at the end of the 1958 season.

Launched at Lorain, Ohio, in 1927, the *Bradley* immediately began setting records for cargo carried. In the summer of 1929 she claimed the record for the largest single cargo ever carried on the Great Lakes: 18,114 tons of limestone.

In November 1958 the *Bradley*, thirty-one years old, was in her prime as a lake boat and was still considered among the giants of the Great Lakes. But as young as she may have been, she was also beginning to show the ravages of her fast, hard life.

There had been reports by the men in the *Bradley*'s crew that the ship had "rust pouring from her hold" and that the ballast tanks leaked constantly. There were also weakened and missing rivets in one ballast tank's interior wall, discovered during a Coast Guard inspection early in 1958. But bolts had been installed in place of the rivets, and the Coast Guard certified the vessel as seaworthy, as did the Lloyd's Register of Shipping Inspection Service.

On Monday, November 17, the *Bradley* unloaded her cargo of limestone in Indiana and at 6:30 P.M. turned back into Lake Michigan and started for home, Rogers City, Michigan, on Lake Huron, a thirty-hour sail away. This was scheduled to be her last trip of the season. Of the thirty-five men aboard the *Bradley*, twenty-six were residents of Rogers City, six were from the northern Michigan area, and three were from out of state.

The weather had been deteriorating for the past two days, with strengthening winds and building seas, but there appeared no reason for concern as the *Bradley*, now with nine thousand tons of water in her ballast tanks to give her stability, plowed through a moderately white-capped lake followed by a southwest wind.

Early Tuesday morning gale warnings were posted for Lake Michigan, sending many ships to safe harbor. But the *Bradley* steamed ahead; most large freighters, used to sailing through heavy weather, do not fear the gales, having confidence in their vessel's ability to withstand a little pounding. Besides, this was their final trip of the year and the crew was anxious to be home.

As dusk approached, the *Brad* was swinging more to an easterly heading as Captain Bryan prepared to thread his way through the passage north of Beaver Island and into the Straits of Mackinac.

At 5:15 P.M., Bryan radioed the Bradley Transportation Line—a division of U.S. Steel—at Rogers City, advising them that he expected to have the ship in at about 2:00 A.M.

The wind had increased to fifty-seven knots (sixty-five miles per hour), and the seas were between twenty and thirty feet high. In these heavy seas the *Bradley*, with only water ballast to keep her rigid, was twisting and bending like a huge snake. Down below, the stresses on the hull were causing rivets to shear off, popping them like bullets from a rifle, and with each lost rivet the hull grew weaker.

At 5:31 P.M., as Captain Bryan stood in the wheelhouse discussing the passage through the Beaver Island archipelago with First Mate Elmer Fleming, a sudden and unusual thud was heard, causing the two officers to look back along the spar deck.

Two-thirds of the way down the deck, illuminated by a string of weather lights running down the center, the men saw the aft section of the boat sag downward.

"She's breaking apart!" Bryan shouted, leaping to the engine telegraph and moving the levers to *ALL STOP*. He then sounded the general alarm, alerting the crew to an emergency.

Within half a minute a second thud came, and the boat appeared to be humping amidships as the stern sagged further.

First Mate Fleming, at the captain's order, grabbed the radiophone and shouted: "Mayday! Mayday! Mayday! This is the *Carl D. Bradley.* Our position is approximately twelve miles southwest of Gull Island. We are in serious trouble."

Captain Bryan was on the ship's intercom system advising the crew to "Run, grab life jackets. Get your life jackets."

"The ship is breaking up in heavy seas," Fleming was broadcasting to a stunned audience of Coast Guard stations and other ships on the lake. "We're breaking up. We're going down!"

Bryan next reached for the ship's whistle and gave the "abandon ship" signal—seven short blasts followed by one long.

A fourth thud came and the *Bradley* jumped, sagged once more, and then split in two. Fleming, giving the Mayday call again, stopped in mid-sentence. It was no longer any use; the power cables had been severed, and the lights and the radio went dead. Radio transmission had halted at exactly 5:45 P.M.

Throughout the two sections of the rapidly sinking vessel, the crew scrambled to get out. Several men attempted to launch the starboard lifeboat on the after section, but the now stern-high deck prevented them from getting it away.

As the forward section began to roll over, the men out on deck were thrown into the frigid, heaving lake. Captain Bryan remained in the wheelhouse. At almost the same moment, the stern half of the boat dived below the surface, her boilers exploding as the icy waters poured in. The *Carl D. Bradley* was gone—the largest vessel ever to be lost on the Great Lakes.

The majority of the crew had jumped or been thrown into the water, and most had managed to don life jackets. But the pounding waves and the freezing wind rapidly sucked the life-giving warmth from their bodies. The water temperature was thirty-six degrees; the air temperature was in the twenties.

As the forward section went down, the forty-two-year-old First Mate Fleming and Frank Mays, a twenty-six-year-old watchman, had been thrown into the water almost on top of the ship's only life raft—a series of empty oil drums topped with an eight-by-ten-foot section of timbers. Crawling aboard, they attempted to reach a hand to other crew members, but the thrashing waters carried them away.

After fruitless attempts at grabbing those struggling in the water, Fleming and Mays managed to bring Gary Strzelecki, a twenty-one-year-old watchman, and twenty-five-year-old Dennis Meredith, a deckhand, onto the raft.

Four miles away, the 250-foot German freighter *Christian Sartori*, under the command of Captain Muller, a former U-boat officer, had heard Fleming's radio distress call and had informed the Coast Guard that he was heading for the scene. Driving into the stiff wind and the oncoming waves, the *Sartori* took two hours to travel the four miles.

Meanwhile, at the Charlevoix, Michigan, Coast Guard station, forty-eight miles from the spot where the *Bradley* had gone down, a thirty-six-foot power launch, manned by three men, put out into the fury of the storm. After an hour of fighting the mountainous seas the boat was recalled, and the 180-foot Coast Guard cutter *Sundew*, a combination buoy tender-icebreaker, set out from the harbor. The *Sundew*'s sister ship, the *Hollhock*, from Sturgeon Bay, Wisconsin, had been on the way to the scene of the *Bradley*'s sinking since the first distress message. The two vessels arrived in the area about eleven o'clock and joined the *Sartori* in a crisscross search for survivors. A Coast Guard aircraft from Traverse City also joined the search, dropping flares over the area to assist the surface vessels.

On the pitching life raft, the four men clung together, trying to coax out a mutual warmth from their sodden, trembling bodies. In the early hours, First Mate Fleming had fired the flares he'd found in the raft's survival kit, saving the last one until a rescue vessel was actually sighted. When a ship did approach through the blackness of the stormy night, the flare failed to fire.

Countless times during the night the waves flicked the bobbing raft out of the water, turning it completely over and throwing the men into the lake, forcing them to struggle for their lives to get back and drag themselves aboard again. After one capsizing, Dennis Meredith failed to return. And just before dawn, Gary Strzelecki, the watchman who had labored valiantly to keep everyone's spirits high throughout the long and wretched night, let his own resolve flag, drifting into a rambling state of semi-consciousness and then shock. He slipped from the raft and was gone, in spite of the efforts of Fleming and Mays to save him.

Mays became very frightened when he noticed that ice had begun to form in his hair and had encrusted his jacket.

"I prayed every minute of the time," he said later. "I felt that, if we were still on the raft by morning, someone would surely find us."

Finally, at daylight, twenty miles and fourteen hours from where the *Carl D. Bradley* had gone down, the cutter *Sundew* picked them out of the water.

The two men refused the offer to fly them by helicopter back to the hospital. Instead, they asked to remain aboard while the search for their shipmates continued. But no other survivors were found. Of the thirty-five men aboard when the boat started back up the lake, thirty-three, including her skipper, failed to make port.

In Rogers City, fifty-five children were left fatherless. Eighteen bodies were recovered. The other fifteen were claimed forever by the tempestuous lake that will not be tamed.

At a joint funeral for the bodies that had been found, held in Rogers City and attended by Protestants and Catholics alike, Monsignor Womicki, bishop of Saginaw, Michigan, voiced the thought that ached in the hearts of all who were there:

"While reaching for the stars and moon, we have not yet mastered our elements of air, water, and fire."

"If Luck Is with Us, This Will Be Our Last Trip"

On November 26, 1966, the 660-foot ore freighter *Daniel J. Morrell* left her home port of Lackawanna, New York, and headed west across Lake Erie. She shouldn't have been on the lake at all, for the 1966 shipping season was supposed to have ended a few days earlier. But the *Morrell's* master, Captain Arthur J. Crawley, had explained to his disappointed crew of thirty-two men that this one last trip to Lake Superior and back was required to fill the tonnage commitments of the Bethlehem Steel Company, the owner of the *Morrell.*

The *Morrell's* sister ship, the *Edward Y. Townsend*, under the command of Thomas J. Connelly, a veteran of twenty-seven years on the lakes, had followed the *Morrell* up the lake from Lackawanna. The two skippers stayed in radio contact as the boats moved north through Lake St. Clair, the St. Clair River, and into Lake Huron, with the *Morrell* a bit more than twenty miles in the lead.

At noon on November 28, the weather bureau was posting gale warnings with northeasterly winds at thirty-four to forty knots the following twelve hours, with snow, or snow and rain, for the next twenty-four hours.

Through the evening Crawley and Connelly conferred as the conditions on Huron steadily worsened. At about ten o'clock in the evening, Connelly considered turning about and returning to Port Huron, but he changed his mind after realizing the danger of falling into a trough in the growing seas and not being able to get out again. The two shipmasters discussed heaving to in the shelter of Thunder Bay.

Dennis Hale had gone off duty at 8:00 P.M. After a hot meal in the after deckhouse crew's mess, he had returned to his room in the fo'c'sle, read for a while, and at about 9:30 had climbed into his bunk, stripped to his underwear.

Hale, twenty-six years old, would be happy to see his third season as a deck watchman on the *Morrell* finally come to an end—damned happy. Although the pay was good, the six-foot, 230-pound father of four disliked the long periods away from home, and he had a nervous respect for the awesome storms that sometimes struck the lakes.

Around eleven o'clock, Crawley called Connelly on the radio. But the *Townsend*'s skipper had his hands full at that moment: his boat was blowing around, broadside to the wind, and Connelly was busy trying to muscle the vessel back on course.

"I'll call you back," Connelly said tersely.

Shortly after midnight on November 29, Connelly, having successfully regained control of his vessel, called Crawley. The *Morrell*'s skipper confided that a similar experience had befallen his boat. The winds at that time were northerly at sixty-five miles an hour, and the seas were running at twenty feet. Crawley signed off with a hopeful "Good luck." It was the last contact the *Townsend* would have with the *Morrell.*

Connelly maintained a constant listening watch on Channel 51—the distress frequency—hearing nothing.

Throughout the remainder of the hellish night, Connelly made repeated attempts to raise the *Morrell* on radio, without success. Concluding that the *Morrell* had experienced radio problems—possibly her antenna had been carried away—Connelly felt no concern. It would not be until 12:15 P.M. on November 30—thirty-six hours after the last communication with the *Morrell*—that the Bethlehem Steel Company's Cleveland office would notify the Coast Guard that the vessel was overdue at the Soo Locks.

The *Daniel J. Morrell* and the *Edward Y. Townsend* were both sixty years of age, built with a type of steel that had not been used after 1948, when it was discovered to be highly brittle at temperatures below the freezing point—temperatures both vessels experienced on Lake Huron in late November 1966.

Dennis Hale, who had finally managed to drift off to sleep despite the terrible din from the howling storm and the ship's rattling equipment, was awakened at about 2:00 A.M. by a new sound. This had an explosive, banging quality that Hale felt as well as heard. He lay in the darkness of his room, wondering about the nature of the noise.

Within a minute of the first crashing sound there came a second, louder, jarring one. At the same instant the books on a shelf over his bed came tumbling down. Hale reached up and flipped the switch on his bunk light, but nothing happened. As he clicked the switch several times, trying to get the light to work, he was startled by the loud clanging of the general alarm bells.

Jumping out of bed, he grabbed a life jacket and dashed into the corridor. No lights burned there, either. At the watertight door leading to the spar deck he bumped into watchman Albert Whoeme, who had arrived an instant before. Whoeme undogged the metal door and peered out.

"Oh, my God!" Whoeme shouted. "Get your life jacket!"

Hale glanced around Whoeme. The lights at the stern were burning brightly, but they stopped about halfway forward. The aft section of the boat appeared to be higher than the forward end.

Hale dashed back to his darkened room, searching for his trousers and shoes—he was wearing only a pair of undershorts—but in the blackness of the rolling, pitching room he was able to locate only his heavy, woolen pea jacket.

Back on the spar deck Hale found the forward crew gathered around the life raft in various stages of dress, none fully prepared for the severe conditions. Hale himself was standing barefoot in a pile of slushy snow.

Getting aft to the lifeboats was impossible. The *Morrell* was being torn in two at hatch eleven: the tortured screaming of tearing metal plates, the showering sparks from severed electrical cables, and the geysering clouds from broken steam lines all attested to that fact.

The life raft, around which thirteen shivering men from the forward section stood, was a pontoon type with a wood-slat floor and wooden sides. It was heavy, but capable of being thrown overboard. However, the men decided that the simplest thing would be for all to get inside the life raft and wait for the bow section to sink out from under them—it would be but a matter of minutes, they knew.

Into the raft went Captain Crawley; First Mate Philip Kapets; Second Mate Duncan McLeod; wheelsmen Henry Richmiller, Stuart Campbell, and Charles Fosbender; watchmen Albert Whoeme, Norman Bragg, Larry Davis, and Dennis Hale; deckhands John Cleary and Arthur Stojeck; and Ernest Marcotta, the *Morrell*'s third mate.

With one final screech of pain, the last fragments of steel connecting the two sections of the vessel parted. The aft section, still under power, forged ahead, bumping and banging into the helpless fore section, pushing it aside. The bow section slowly slipped around until it had fully reversed its course. The men on deck watched in stunned silence as the stern half of the *Morrell* moved past, still making steam and ablaze with lights as it churned away into the darkness without a helm to guide it, leaving them alone in the howling storm. It would only be a matter of time, they knew, before the aft section, taking on water from the gaping hole where the two sections had been joined, would slip beneath the waves as even now the forward section was doing.

The men waited for the deck to sink out from beneath them, but a thunderous wave struck the wallowing hulk as it dipped slowly downward and swept the men and raft over the side, spiraling down into the freezing lake. Hale came to the surface, gasping against the shock of the extreme cold, within arm's reach of the bobbing raft. By the time he had managed to crawl aboard, deckhands Stojeck and Cleary were already in the raft. Between the three of them they managed to pull one other man into the raft—Charles Fosbender, a wheelsman. None of the other men were in sight.

Fosbender was the only one of the four in the raft who was fully clothed—he had finished his watch at midnight and had not yet gone to his cabin when the *Morrell* broke apart.

Hale, going through the raft's emergency kit, found— in addition to a signal pistol, six amber flares, six parachute flares, and a sea anchor—a can of storm oil. He planned to spread the heavy oil over his nearly naked body to help protect it from the cold wind and water, but before he could, one of the others, thinking it was useless, tossed it overboard.

Hale fired the flares, spacing them over several hours. No one saw any of them. The men were alone in one savage corner of Lake Huron.

Through the seemingly endless night they huddled together, trying to keep warm. Before dawn John Cleary and Arthur Stojeck had died, robbed of their precious body heat and the vital will to live.

Through the day of Tuesday, November 29, Fosbender grew steadily weaker, complaining that his lungs were filling with water.

"I told him to crawl near me," Hale said later.

As he did, he raised himself in the raft and shouted that he saw land through a break in the clouds of snow that swirled around them. Periodically, Fosbender would lift himself up to look hopefully for signs of life, of rescue. He saw none. Finally, he quietly died.

Through the rest of the day and all of Tuesday night, Hale, the former hotel cook who had never really enjoyed sailing, fought a grim and unyielding battle with death. At times he thought he could see the lights of farmhouses on shore. But his feet were now frozen, and if the raft did somehow beach itself on or near the water's edge, Hale knew he would never be able to crawl to safety.

He burrowed himself beneath the stiff corpses of his shipmates for whatever warmth and protection from the elements they might provide, all the while drifting in and out of consciousness.

During Wednesday afternoon, his feet and one hand now frozen, his hair caked with ice, his body writhing in pain, Dennis Hale came fully awake. He felt hungry and thirsty and began halfheartedly eating bits of ice that he plucked from his jacket.

Suddenly there was someone else with him on the raft—an old man with long, white hair and heavy eyebrows and a moustache; his complexion was an eerie milk white

color, and his eyes were commanding. The elderly appari-
tion grimly warned Hale against eating the ice.

Hale dropped into another period of semiconscious-
ness, and when he awoke he again picked at the icicles on
his jacket, putting them in his mouth and chewing them.
Again the old man appeared and, more forcefully this
time, lectured Dennis: "I told you not to eat the ice off
your coat. It will lower your body temperature and you'll
die." Hale drifted once more into a stupor, only slightly
aware of his surroundings.

On Wednesday morning, the *Townsend*, as pre-
viously instructed by the Cleveland office, docked at Lime
Island in the St. Marys River below the Soo Locks to take
on fuel. Captain Connelly still was of the impression that
the *Morrell* was somewhere ahead, perhaps experiencing
radio difficulties.

Meanwhile, in Cleveland, Chief Dispatcher Arthur
Dobson had become increasingly concerned about two of
his ships. The reporting station at the Soo had failed to
mention the arrival of either the *Morrell* or the *Townsend*.
He put in a call to the Coast Guard asking for information
about either vessel. The Coast Guard located the *Townsend* in the St. Marys River. The *Morrell*, Dobson was told,
could not be found.

At about the time Dobson was making his call to the
Soo, the motor vessel *G. G. Post* reported sighting a body
floating off Harbor Beach, in Michigan's "thumb" area.

Less than an hour later, the freighter *G. A. Tomlinson*
spotted three more bodies and wreckage about four miles
north-northeast of where the first body had been seen. All
wore life jackets with *Morrell* markings. It now became
clear that the *Daniel J. Morrell* would not be arriving at
the Soo.

A massive air-sea search was mounted: planes, helicopters, and surface vessels swarmed over the area. Meanwhile, ground parties were patrolling the snowy beaches, looking for bodies that may have washed ashore. The *Morrell*'s aft life raft was found unoccupied, but with a body trapped and submerged underneath.

At about four o'clock Wednesday afternoon, a Coast Guard helicopter sighted a life raft south of Harbor Beach. A crew member, checking the raft with binoculars, informed the pilot that the raft carried four dead bodies— "They're all frozen stiff." The Coast Guard helicopter pilot eased the aircraft down onto the surface of the now relatively calm lake, directly against the quietly undulating raft. Just as the crewman stepped aboard to begin unstacking the bodies, a right arm raised weakly and Dennis Hale lifted his head.

A Coast Guard officer in the helicopter radioed that Hale was "in minor shock but in amazingly good condition." Doctors in Harbor Beach found his body temperature to be 95 degrees—3.6 degrees below normal. Asked how the burly sailor could have survived the grueling ordeal and murderous conditions, one examining physician replied, "He's twenty-six and he didn't panic. But it's still a miracle."

An additional twenty of the dead *Morrell* crew were eventually recovered from the lake. Eight were never found. Hale alone survived.

A Coast Guard board of investigation concluded that the *Morrell* suffered "brittle fracture" of its hull caused by prolonged twisting and bending in water whose temperature was sufficiently low to promote fracturing of the steel.

The *Townsend* reported a crack in her plates near the number twelve hatch that extended down to the shear strake. (Hale recalls the *Morrell* splitting in two at about the same location.) A Coast Guard inspector, after viewing the crack, ordered the *Townsend* towed to the nearest shipyard. It was never again allowed to carry cargo, and several years later it was sold to a Spanish scrap company. It broke apart and sank while being towed across the Atlantic Ocean.

Dennis Hale suffered severe frostbite to several toes, but otherwise came away from his nightmarish ordeal in remarkably good condition, physically. He suffered a greater form of torture as the result of his experience on Lake Huron in November 1966.

Great Lakes sailors who have survived the disaster of losing their boat and their crewmates speak of the "why you syndrome," a malady that manifests itself most painfully when they meet the wives or families of their shipmates who didn't survive. Whether spoken or not, whether real or imagined, these men see in the eyes of the bereaved the unmistakable question, Why you? Why did you live instead of my loved one?

Hale never went back on the lakes. When last heard of, he was working as a machinist in Ohio, never wanting to discuss his memories or to relive his nightmare.

The day after she was given the news that her husband's body had been recovered from the raft on which Dennis Hale had so miraculously clung to life, Jan Fosbender received a letter at her St. Clair, Michigan, home. It was from her dead husband. It had been dropped to the mail boat *J. W. Wescott* as the *Morrell* steamed up the Detroit River on the way to its rendezvous with extinction. The letter closed with this eerily ironic inscription: "If luck is with us, this will be our last trip."

THE BELL TOLLS TWENTY-NINE TIMES

Sunday, November 9, 1975, was a beautiful day in the Duluth, Minnesota/Superior, Wisconsin metropolitan area. The temperature had been unseasonably warm, and everyone seemed anxious to be outdoors for what would probably be the last pleasant day before the harsh, bitter winter set in.

Shortly before seven that morning, the ore freighter *Edmund Fitzgerald* had slipped into the harbor and made for the Burlington-Northern ore docks on the Superior side of the port. There she was to receive a cargo of 26,116 long tons of taconite ore pellets.

The flagship of the Oglebay-Norton Company of Cleveland, the *Fitzgerald* was one of the most recognized and admired of all the iron boats. Measuring 729 feet from stem to stern, she was the largest vessel on the Great Lakes when she was launched near Detroit in 1958. Shore dwellers near the lakes knew the *"Fitz"* and her crew well—she was a sturdy, reliable, comfortable boat manned by the best sailors on the lakes.

Several of those sailors were contemplating retirement, including Captain Ernest "Mac" McSorley, a forty-four-year veteran of the lakes who loved the *Fitzgerald* but who also had an ailing wife back home in Toledo. Still, he hoped to get in "just a few more seasons."

Jack McCarthy, the sixty-two-year-old first mate, had once been a skipper himself, but in 1956 he had put his boat on the rocks near Sandusky Bay. Now he was looking to close out his career with dignity.

Cook Robert Rafferty, also sixty-two, had at first liked his temporary assignment on the *Fitz*. He was filling in for the regular cook, who was sick ashore with bleeding ulcers. But recently Bob had been having premonitions of disaster: "Get off this boat as soon as you can," he had blurted to a crewman on November 8.

First Engineer Eddie Bindon, only forty-seven, had nevertheless already made up his mind to retire as soon as the *Fitzgerald* wintered up. The fierce November storms on the lakes made him more and more nervous as each year passed; besides, his beloved uncle Joe was dying of cancer.

At approximately 1:15 P.M. the last pocket of taconite pellets was emptied into the number eleven hatch. During the loading process the *Fitzgerald*'s fuel tanks had been topped off with 50,013 gallons of No. 6 fuel oil. As soon as the loading had been completed, First Mate McCarthy called for the draft readings fore and aft. The bow had a reading of twenty-seven feet, two inches, and the draft at the rudder was twenty-seven feet, six inches. At 1:52 P.M., the *Fitzgerald* steamed past the breakwater and into Lake Superior, headed for Detroit.

At 3:39 P.M. the National Weather Service announced the raising of gale warnings on Lake Superior, forecasting winds of thirty-four to thirty-eight knots. A "fringe gale," many ships' officers called it, not unusual at that time of the year.

A few minutes earlier, the 767-foot U.S. Steel ore carrier *Arthur M. Anderson* steamed out of Two Harbors, Minnesota, with a load of taconite pellets for the giant steel-making complex at Gary, Indiana.

In the charthouse, a pipe wedged firmly between his teeth, stood Captain Jesse "Bernie" Cooper, a soft-spoken North Carolinian with thirty-eight years of sailing experience, including a harrowing night on Lake Michigan during the blow of 1940.

Looking out the chartroom windows, Cooper could see, about fifteen miles astern and to starboard, an ore boat, obviously coming out of the Duluth area. Grabbing a radiotelephone handset, he called the boat, asking the identification of the vessel. The boat answered, "This is *Edmund Fitzgerald*."

Cooper knew McSorley, the *Fitz*'s skipper, and immediately suggested that since gale warnings had been posted, the two boats might stay together and "run the northern track" across Superior to "get over to the north shore for shelter in case it really starts to blow." McSorley agreed. It was always better to have company, particularly if there was the possibility of heavy weather.

By 7:00 P.M., winds on the lake were picking up. A slight chop was developing, and an occasional gust sent up on the *Fitzgerald's* spar deck a frothy spray that streamed along the hatch combings before the scuppers carried it back to the lake.

At 10:39 P.M. the marine forecaster in Chicago revised his projection for Lake Superior, predicting: "Easterly winds 32 to 42 knots becoming southwesterly Monday morning, and west to southwest 35 to 45 knots Monday afternoon, rain and thunderstorms, waves 5 to 10 feet increasing to 8 to 15 feet Monday."

At 1:00 A.M. on November 10, the *Edmund Fitzgerald*, a designated weather-reporting vessel, radioed its scheduled report, detailing the conditions at its present location. The *Fitz* was twenty-three miles south of Isle Royale's Siskiwit Bay and thirty-eight miles west of Eagle Harbor on Michigan's Keweenaw Peninsula. A heavy rain had dropped visibility on the lake to between two and four miles. Waves were ten feet high and the winds were north-northeast at fifty-two knots (sixty miles an hour).

In the Chicago office of the National Weather Service, the marine forecaster took the *Fitzgerald's* report and added the information to the data coming in from other vessels on the lake, weather satellite photos, and sequence reports from the other weather-service offices. Working steadily he prepared a "Special Weather Bulletin" that would be broadcast on radio frequencies 162.55 megahertz and 162.40 megahertz at 2:00 A.M.: "Change gale warnings to storm warnings immediately."

At 7:00 A.M. the *Fitzgerald's* position was 58 miles north of Copper Harbor, Michigan. The winds at this position were from the northeast at thirty-five knots, down from the fifty-two knots reported at 1:00 A.M. due to the boat's proximity to the Canadian shore and to an overall moderation in the storm's activity as its center passed over Marquette, Michigan. A light rain was falling and visibility was two to four miles. Wave heights remained at ten feet, but the *Fitz*, heavily laden with ore pellets, was "working well" in the seas, with little pitching and almost no rolling.

The *Arthur M. Anderson* was then a few miles astern—the faster *Fitzgerald* had overtaken and passed the U.S. Steel ore boat at about three o'clock that morning.

At 7:00 A.M. Captain McSorley placed a radiotelephone call from the *Fitzgerald* to Oglebay-Norton's Cleveland office: "Our ETA (estimated time of arrival) at the Soo is indefinite because of the weather," he said.

Shortly after 8:00 A.M. on November 10, Raymond R. Waldman, meteorologist in charge of the National Weather Forecast Office in Chicago, arrived at work. "It's shaping up to be a good-sized storm," said George Polensky, the supervisor who had earlier that morning issued the storm warnings, upgrading the conditions from a gale. Waldman glanced at the data coming in from reporting stations throughout the nation, nodded agreement, and then, thinking back over his thirty-three years' experience with Great Lakes weather, said, "We've had worse."

At 9:53 A.M., Captain Cooper of the *Anderson* conferred by radiophone with Captain McSorley.

"The seas are moderating considerably," Cooper said. "I think we could head due east."

McSorley agreed, and the two boats turned to a ninety-degree heading. The *Fitzgerald* was slowly pulling ahead of the *Anderson* and shortly before 10:00 A.M. was about twenty-five miles south of the Slate Islands, off the north shore of Lake Superior. The winds were holding out of the north-northeast at twenty-six knots. The seas were down somewhat, with some heavy spray coming over the decks but no "green water"—heavy boarding waves.

"Hold this course until you can make for Otter Head with the wind at our stern," McSorley told Second Mate James Pratt. "Stay off about three miles from the Otter Head light."

At noon the *Fitzgerald* was between two and three miles northwest of Otter Head light on the eastern shore of Ontario. Winds were out of the southwest and had dropped to eleven knots. The barometer was down to 28.82 inches. They were in the eye of the storm.

The wind would be "hauling around" out of the northwest soon and would increase, McSorley knew. He wanted to be beyond the Michipicoten light, on the Ontario shore, before the seas began to build under the change in winds.

McSorley, from years of experience, was prepared to have the seas run "funny" down through the passage when the winds came from the northwest. He wanted to make his turn at just the right time to have the wind on his stern.

The *Fitzgerald* was equipped with two surface-scan radar units: one of small scale—which provided greater magnification of detail but at a more limited distance—and one of large scale—which covered a greater distance, but offered less fine detail of features. The large-scale radar set had begun to malfunction periodically in the early hours of the morning and had been shut down. During McSorley's call to Cleveland earlier that morning, he asked that a technician meet the boat in Detroit to correct the problem.

In addition to the small-scale radar, the *Fitzgerald* could also use its radio direction finder to home in on Lake Superior radio beacons to assist in plotting their exact location.

Meanwhile, in the *Anderson*'s chartroom, Bernie Cooper was looking at the concentric arcs of barometric pressure known as isobars that he had drawn on his lake chart. He was astonished at what he saw. A better than average weather forecaster in his own right, Cooper rechecked his figures, not believing what they had told him. He must have made a mistake, he thought. According to his estimates, the back side of the storm now passing overhead would generate winds from the northwest with speeds of eighty knots. Bernie Cooper would later discover that his wind speed forecast would be more accurate than that of the National Weather Service.

The weather satellite photographs transmitted to the National Weather Service during the afternoon of November 10 clearly portrayed the massive weather system that gripped the eastern one-third of the United States. The swirling counterclockwise circulation of clouds spread over all of Michigan, Wisconsin, Minnesota, Illinois, Indiana, and Ohio; parts of Pennsylvania, New York, and the northeastern seaboard; and much of the Tennessee Valley. Trails of the system extended all the way down to the Florida Keys.

The weather on Lake Superior was in an agitated state of flux. At one o'clock in the afternoon the motor vessel *Simcoe*, ten miles southwest of the *Fitzgerald*, reported winds from the west at forty-four knots, with waves of seven feet. The Whitefish Point weather station had the winds from the south-southeast at nineteen knots, gusting to thirty-four, while the Stannard Rock station, north of Marquette, reported winds from the west-northwest at fifty knots, gusting to fifty-nine. The regular afternoon forecast from the National Weather Service in Chicago predicted "Northwest winds thirty-eight to fifty-two knots with gusts to sixty knots early tonight."

At about 1:40 P.M. Captain Cooper talked with McSorley. "I'm going to haul to the west for a while," Cooper said, indicating he wanted to alter his course to run farther beyond the west end of Michipicoten Island to put the anticipated wind change directly on his stern.

"Well, I'm rolling some, but I think I'll hold this course until I'm ready to turn for Caribou," McSorley had replied.

The *Fitzgerald* at this time was nine miles ahead of the *Anderson*. The *Fitz* was extending its lead by virtue of its more direct approach to the passage between Michipicoten and Caribou islands. The lead would extend to seventeen miles, miles that also marked a separation in time—minutes between them that would become precious, lost minutes that would not be recovered.

Michipicoten Island is located one hundred and six miles northwest of Sault Ste. Marie and twenty-five miles due west of the Canadian shoreline. It is a rocky, largely barren landmass measuring seventeen miles east to west and five miles north to south. Twenty-two miles to the south is Caribou Island, an even more desolate piece of real estate measuring three miles north to south and approximately one and a half miles east to west.

In between the islands the depth of the water ranges from one hundred fathoms (six hundred feet) to a shallow area north and east of Caribou Island known as Six Fathom Shoal.

Mariners sailing these waters rely on two basic sets of navigational charts to find their way across Lake Superior: U.S. Chart L.S. 9 and Canadian Chart 2310. Both sets of maps are periodically updated to reflect changes in the topography of the region (new shoreline installations such as navigation lights or radio beacons, newly created harbors, etc.) and also to identify possible hazards to navigation (wrecked vessels, newly discovered shoal areas, etc.)

Both the American and the Canadian charts in use on November 10, 1975, indicated the Six Fathom Shoal, also denoted as North Bank. Both based the location and depth of the shallow waters on the Canadian Hydrographic Service surveys of 1916 and 1919. But the location of the shoal on U.S. Chart L.S. 9 was different from that shown on Canadian Chart 2310, with the U.S. chart placing Six Fathom Shoal approximately 350 feet farther south and a third of a mile east of the position indicated for the shallows on Canadian Chart 2310.

However, both charts were inaccurate as to location and *depth*. Rather than 6 fathoms (36 feet), the shoal was actually 4.1 fathoms (24.6 feet). The *Fitzgerald*, loaded with 26,116 tons of taconite pellets, drew a little over 27 feet.

An overcast sky hung low over the eastern end of Lake Superior as the *Fitzgerald* came around the point of Michipicoten Island, putting the West End Light directly on her port beam. The winds were swinging around, coming from the west-northwest, and were down to a pleasant five knots.

At 2:45 in the afternoon, the *Fitzgerald* was about eleven miles due south of Michipicoten Island, holding a 141-degree heading. The winds had come around and were now out of the northwest at forty-three knots and increasing. The seas were running sixteen feet and building rapidly. The boat continued working well in the growing seas, the wind now almost directly on her stern. A heavy snow had begun falling, reducing visibility to near zero.

McSorley had ordered a course change just before two o'clock, plotting the trackline to take the *Fitzgerald* to a point about five miles off the northern tip of Caribou Island. The plot for this trackline depended on accurately pinpointing the boat's position at the time the turn to 141 degrees was made. But, the malfunctioning large-scale radar had been shut down, and the increasing sea return showing up on the Sperry Mark 3 (the small-scale radar) made the radar bearings from Caribou Island unreliable. Consequently, the vessel was farther to the west than they believed when the turn to 141 degrees was made. The *Fitzgerald* was heading directly for the Six Fathom Shoal.

Aboard the *Anderson*, a solemn gathering was taking place around the boat's radar consoles. Captain Cooper, First Mate Morgan E. Clark, and Second Mate Roy T. Anderson were looking at a white dot showing up on each of their two receivers.

"Look at this, Morgan," Cooper said, indicating the dot. "He's in close to that six-fathom."

The dot the three men were watching so intently was a radar "target" that represented the *Edmund Fitzgerald*.

"He sure looks like he's in that shoal area," Clark responded.

"He sure does," Cooper said. "He's closer than I'd want this ship to be."

As the *Fitzgerald* labored through the growing seas, the water depth beneath her hull was rising sharply from over two hundred feet to less than thirty. The men on the bridge were totally unaware of this since the *Fitzgerald*, like almost every other lake boat, was not equipped with a Fathometer, a device that measured and displayed the depth of the water under a boat's keel. The Coast Guard had determined that since most lake boats were commanded by men who had sailed the Great Lakes for most of their lives, shipmasters would know where the dangerous shallows were located. Therefore the two hundred dollar piece of electronics gear was not required.

At some point as the *Fitz* passed over the shoals, rising and falling in the rolling waves, she probably crashed down on a rocky peak, smashing in a portion of the starboard hull at frames sixty-eight, sixty-nine, and seventy in E strake (strakes divide the hull on a horizontal line along the boat's sides), at the point where ballast tanks three and four joined.

The sudden pressure of the inward movement of plates, compressing the trapped air in the tanks, caused two ballast-tank vents located on the spar deck to blow out. At the same time, the violent pressure increase, or possibly a piece of the broken hull plates, tore a hole in the side of the tanks, which shared a common wall with the cargo holds.

At about the same instant, a towering wave smashed into the stern of the boat, rolling along the spar deck and crashing against the forward superstructure.

On the bridge, Captain McSorley and First Mate Mc-Carthy checked the deck for possible damage by the huge wave. They noted that two ballast-tank vents were blown from their deck welds and that a section of the steel-cable railing had been torn away.

Almost immediately, the *Fitzgerald* began listing slightly to starboard. It was a lethal flood.

The two lost vent covers allowed water coming on deck to pour into the two tanks, giving the false impression that this was the cause of the list.

"Start the auxiliary pumps," McSorley had ordered Chief Engineer George Holl, who immediately had both two-thousand-gallon-per-minute pumps started and switched on the necessary valves to begin drawing water from the two tanks and to pump it back into Lake Superior. These two pumps should have been enough to remove any water coming into the tanks from two torn eighteen-inch-diameter vents.

McSorley grabbed the radiophone handset from its cradle on the forward wheelhouse bulkhead.

"*Arthur M. Anderson*, this is the *Fitzgerald*. I have sustained some topside damage; I have some fence rail laid down, two vents lost or damaged, and I have taken a list. I am checking down [slowing the boat]. Will you stay by me until I get down [into Whitefish Bay]?"

"This is the *Anderson*, ah, Charlie on that [I understand]. Do you have your pumps going?" Cooper asked.

"Yes," came McSorley's reply. "Both of them."

The *Fitzgerald* had, in addition to the two-thousand-gallon-per-minute pumps, four electrically driven seven-thousand-gallon-per-minute main ballast pumps.

Captain Cooper assured McSorley that he would make every effort to catch the *Fitzgerald* and stay close by. "I knew he was too close," Cooper said later. "He was right in those shoals."

Over the next forty minutes, with the *Fitzgerald* twisting and turning in the heavy seas, the tear in the hull was growing, allowing more and more lake water to pour into the ballast tanks and from there into the cargo hold.

Water in the ballast tanks could be pumped, but water entering the cargo hold could not be gotten rid of when the boat was loaded. The only cargo-hold drain was a floor sump located in the aftermost part of cargo hold number three. The taconite pellets effectively blocked that drain, much as hair or other material will stop up a bathtub drain.

At about 4:00 P.M. a sudden gust of wind tore the radar antennae from their masts atop the wheelhouse, hurling them over the bow into the grinding lake. The one functioning radar scope went blank.

"Could you provide me with radar plots?" McSorley asked the *Anderson.*

Captain Cooper was not on the bridge at the time, but First Mate Morgan Clark readily agreed.

"Certainly. I'll keep you advised of your position," Clark replied.

For additional navigational information, the *Fitzgerald* turned to its radio direction finder, homing in on the beacon sending a signal from the Whitefish Point remote RDF station. But fifteen minutes later the Morse code signal from Whitefish Point suddenly clicked off.

Strong winds had blown down the power lines that operated the station. A special backup gasoline-powered generator failed to take over as it was designed to do because an automatic relay—costing a few dollars—stuck at that precise moment, leaving the station inoperative and the *Fitzgerald* blind, totally dependent on the guidance coming from the *Anderson*.

At approximately 4:39 P.M., Gary Wigen, a radioman stationed at the Grand Marais (Michigan) Coast Guard station, received a radio call from the *Fitzgerald*.

"Is the radio beacon at Whitefish Point operating?"

"Stand by. We don't have the equipment here to tell if it's operating properly. I will call you back."

Wigen contacted the Sault Ste. Marie Coast Guard station and was told that their monitoring equipment indicated the beacon and light at the point were both inoperative.

Wigen relayed the information to the *Fitzgerald*.

"Okay, thanks. We were just wondering because we haven't been able to get it for a while."

On Lake Superior, the winds howling through the *Fitzgerald*'s rigging reached eighty miles an hour and were still increasing.

By five o'clock it had become undeniable that there was something much more seriously wrong with the *Fitzgerald* than two broken tank vents.

The king gauges in the engine room showed that water was still coming into ballast tanks three and four; the list had not been corrected, in fact it had gotten worse. Water had to be getting into the cargo holds and building up there, slowly pulling the boat lower and lower in the lake. There was no way around it: sooner or later the *Edmund Fitzgerald* would sink.

Ernest McSorley, forty-four years a sailor, master of one of the proudest ships ever to sail the Great Lakes, stood at the window of the pilothouse looking out at the convulsing lake slowly clawing at his vessel and lamentably admitted to himself that there was the ever-growing possibility that he would lose his boat.

What options did they have available?

They couldn't abandon ship: in this terrible storm, launching lifeboats would be impossible, they would be crushed against the side of the boat or capsized the minute they touched the churning water. The same was true for the two life rafts carried on the boat.

They couldn't don life jackets and jump into the lake: the temperature of the water at that time was forty-seven degrees. Tests conducted later demonstrated that a human body immersed in forty-seven-degree water would go into shock from hypothermia and die within a half hour.

They couldn't SOS the *Anderson*, or any other ship for that matter. Even if a vessel could reach them in time, there was no practical way to transfer the crew from one ship to another given the current conditions.

That only left pushing ahead, hoping the boat would stay afloat long enough to reach the shelter of Whitefish Bay, where it could be beached and the men gotten off safely.

There is every reason to believe that McSorley firmly believed that there was a good possibility that his beloved boat would come through even this storm. But the strain on him was evident in a radio conversation he had with Captain Cedric Woodard, the Great Lakes pilot aboard the *Avafors* in Whitefish Bay.

Although Woodard had known McSorley for quite a while, the voice on the radio did not resemble his friend's voice at all. Knowing he was speaking to the *Fitzgerald*, he asked who he was speaking to. The answer came back, "This is Captain McSorley." Woodard was stunned, but thought that perhaps his friend was very tired or possibly had a cold.

At 5:30 P.M. Woodard called the *Fitzgerald* to let McSorley know that he was just passing the Whitefish Point light on his way out into the lake and that the beacon light had suddenly come on and begun to rotate.

"I'm glad to hear it," McSorley replied, an obvious tone of relief in his voice.

"What are the conditions like up where you are?" Woodard asked.

"We are taking heavy seas over our decks; it's the worst sea I've ever been in. We have a bad list and no radar."

Woodard thought, and then responded, "If I'm correct, you have two radars."

"They're both gone," McSorley said.

At 7:10, Morgan Clark called from the *Anderson* to advise McSorley that he had picked up a target on radar coming out of Whitefish Bay nine miles from the *Fitzgerald* and, in answer to McSorley's question, responded that they would clear each other as long as the *Fitz* held to its present course.

Then, as an afterthought, Clark asked, "By the way, how are you making out with your problems?"

McSorley responded cryptically, "We are holding our own."

It was the last anyone would hear from the *Edmund Fitzgerald.*

A heavy snow squall struck the lake just then and Clark could no longer see the *Fitzgerald*'s running lights. The radar scope was, as he would later describe it, "a white blob."

Captain Cooper—who had been out of the wheelhouse during the last radio contact with McSorley, returned a minute or two later.

At 7:25, the snow abruptly stopped and visibility was unlimited. The men in the *Anderson*'s wheelhouse could see the lights of three upbound vessels.

"We should be able to see the *Fitzgerald*," Clark said.

But they couldn't see her. The upbound ships were clearly visible, and they were at least seventeen miles away. The *Fitzgerald* had been half that distance.

Checking the radar screens they were able to spot the three vessels coming out of the bay, but there was no target that could possibly be the *Fitz*. She had vanished!

The tension in the *Anderson*'s wheelhouse increased as the minutes wore on and no sign of the *Fitzgerald* could be found. Bernie Cooper and Morgan Clark alternated calling the boat on radio but received no reply.

Finally Cooper, to check his equipment, called the freighter *William Clay Ford*, anchored in Whitefish Bay. The *Ford* replied that the *Anderson*'s signal was loud and clear. Cooper then asked if the *Fitzgerald* might have slipped into the bay and was told that it had not.

A feeling of horror gripped the men in the wheelhouse: the possibility that the *Fitzgerald*—the huge ore boat that had been with them throughout the voyage across the storm-tossed lake—had met with disaster was growing rapidly.

At 7:54 P.M., Cooper called Group Soo, the Coast Guard unit at Sault Ste. Marie, and was told to watch for a missing sixteen-foot private motorboat. Cooper and Clark continued trying to raise the *Fitzgerald* on radio and kept a close watch on the radar screens, without success.

Finally, at 8:32, Cooper again radioed Group Soo.

"This is the *Anderson*. I am very concerned with the welfare of the steamer *Edmund Fitzgerald*. He was right in front, experiencing a little difficulty. He was taking on a small amount of water, and none of the upbound ships have passed him. I can see no lights as before, and I don't have him on radar. I just hope he didn't take a nose dive."

This time the Coast Guard took interest and made their own attempts to contact the *Fitzgerald*, again without success.

By 9:15 a full sea and air search had been ordered. Because there were no Coast Guard boats immediately available that were large enough to steam into the storm

or close enough to get to the area soon enough, the Coast
Guard asked commercial vessels anchored in Whitefish
Bay to leave the safety of the sheltered bay and go out into
the stormy lake to look for survivors. Cooper reluctantly
agreed to hazard his vessel and crew, as did the commander of the *William Clay Ford*.

Through the long, frightening night the two ships
crisscrossed the area of the *Fitzgerald*'s last known position. As dawn approached, bits and pieces of flotsam
began to be sighted by the prowling *Arthur M. Anderson*:
a piece of life jacket, an oar, a life ring, a propane cylin-
der, the severely damaged number two lifeboat, and a
sixteen-foot section of the forward part of the number one
lifeboat. No survivors were found; no bodies were recovered.

Jesse Cooper stood in the wheelhouse of the *Anderson* leaning against the forward windows, his body slump-
ing over, his eyes burning, and his mouth and throat dry.

"We're now in the area of debris," he wearily said into
the radiophone. "This is the spot."

Outside, the inky blackness of predawn closed more
tightly around the ship, the sound of the wind now chang-
ing from an enraged shriek to a melancholy moan, as if a
ghostly choir—composed of all the mariners ever claimed
by Lake Superior—was chanting a dirge of grief for the
twenty-nine men newly recruited to their ranks.

The remnants of the mighty *Fitzgerald* were found
the following year by a remote-controlled, camera-
equipped underwater survey vehicle. It lies in two sections
in 530 feet of water. The 276-foot forward section sits
upright, while the 253-foot after section is upside down
170 feet away. The remaining 200 feet of the vessel is
scattered between the two sections.

Each year, on the anniversary of the sinking of the

Edmund Fitzgerald, while a deacon standing in Detroit's Mariner's Cathedral reads aloud the names of the crew members, the old ship's bell in the belfry tolls twenty-nine times.

While the loss of the *Fitzgerald* and its twenty-nine-man crew remains in the memories of countless devotees of Great Lakes history, the great storm of 1913 with more than 250 men and women killed and a dozen large ships sunk is left largely to scholars and researchers. Perhaps the reason for this oversight lies in the fact that the *Fitz* was the last large freighter to be claimed by the bellicose waters of the Great Lakes. No major vessel has gone down in the lakes since it did in 1975.

However, the questions remain: can a terrible November storm happen again, and could we ever again experience the monumental tragedy of losing as many lives as were lost in 1913 or have so many proud ships sucked to the bottom of the lakes? The answer to the first question is yes. The second answer is, probably not. The advances in sophisticated technology, in ship building, in weather forecasting, in communications, and in lifesaving capabilities have far outdistanced what was available in 1913.

Still, other monster storms will strike the Great Lakes when the gales of November come early; there will most certainly be other lives lost; and it is possible there will be more ships gone missing.

Bibliography

BOOKS

Barcus, Frank. *Freshwater Fury*. Detroit, Michigan: Wayne State University Press, 1960.

Bowen, Dana Thomas. *Lore of the Lakes*. Daytona Beach, Florida: Dana Thomas Bowen, 1940.

Boyer, Dwight. *True Tales of the Great Lakes*. New York: Dodd, Mead & Company, 1971.

Dills, Michael, and John Greenwood. *Greenwood's and Dills' Lake Boats '73*. Cleveland: Freshwater Press, 1973.

Hemming, Robert J. *Gales of November: The Sinking of the* Edmund Fitzgerald. Chicago: Contemporary Books, Inc., 1981.

Ratigan, William. *Great Lakes Shipwrecks and Survivals*. Grand Rapids, Michigan: William B. Eerdmans Publishing Co., 1977.

ARTICLES

American Heritage magazine, October/November 1984.

The Blade (Toledo, Ohio), October 21, 29, 30, 1913; November 9–17, 1913.

Chicago Record-Herald, October 29, 1913; November 10, 1913.

Daily Observer (Sarnia, Ontario), November 7–23, 1913.

Detroit Free Press, November 9–17, 1913.

Detroit News, November 9–19, 1913.
Duluth Herald, October 10, 22, 24, 27, 29, 1913; November 9, 15, 1913.

Inland Seas magazine, Summer 1987, number 2; Fall 1988, number 3.

Lake Carrier's Association Annual Report, 1913.

The Signal (Goderich, Ontario), November 13, 20, 27, 1913.

Index